MERSEY MINIS

VOLUME ONE

LANDING

Det

Mersey Minis

VOLUME ONE: LANDING

Edited by Deborah Mulhearn
Illustrations by Clare Curtis
Graphic design by Ken Ashcroft
Printed and bound in Italy at Graphicom

ISBN: 978-0-9548431-7-5

First published in April 2007 by Capsica Ltd
83 Ampthill Road, Liverpool L17 9QN, UK

email: merseyminis@capsica.net
www.merseyminis.com
www.loveliverpoolbooks.com

CONTENTS

Dedicated to
Thomas Joachim Mulhearn
(1927-1991)

INTRODUCTION

LANDING is the first volume of Mersey Minis, a series of small books celebrating Liverpool's 800th anniversary.

Bursting with brilliant writing inspired by Liverpool and the River Mersey, LANDING includes writers ranging from the extremely famous to the completely unknown, from well-loved novelists to young arrivals, from poets and princes to maidservants. What they have in common is Liverpool. Some of the writers were born in the city, others are strangers passing through, or experiencing their first footfall in Europe. But they have all visited or lived in (and in one notable exception merely dreamed about) Liverpool, and, luckily for us, committed their impressions to paper.

The notion of bringing all this amazing output together into one series was irresistible. It seemed a simple enough idea, but as I started digging deeper, I was awed by the sheer volume and variety of people who had recorded their time in Liverpool. There was enough material for a shelf full of books, and how to select and present it all became the challenge. LANDING is about first impressions, new encounters, beginnings, meetings and openings particular to Liverpool. They are funny, fascinating, touching, churlish, bemused, sad, or downright surreal, but all memorable accounts of this singular city and the often quixotic experiences it offers.

The extracts in LANDING are taken from works of fiction, reportage, travel writing, essays, letters and memoirs, and reach right back to Liverpool's beginnings. Much of it is readily accessible but more has languished in archives and libraries. Some extracts are published here for the first time.

The writers' biographies at the back of the book reveal a little bit more about who they were and why they came to Liverpool, and the book list will hopefully prompt further reading about these people who have their own fascinating stories to tell, in which Liverpool has played a part.

Though I am a born and bred Liverpudlian, LANDING has been a thrilling journey of my own. I have seen Liverpool anew and learned much about my city I didn't know before. I hope you enjoy reading LANDING as much as I have enjoyed putting it together.

DEBORAH MULHEARN

A NOTE ON THE TEXT

The extracts in Mersey Minis are reproduced from original sources, many of which are historic and therefore sometimes using styles and language unfamiliar to modern readers. I have, however, in most cases retained the original spellings, punctuation and sometimes the grammatical mistakes so as not to impede the energy and flow of the writer, and to reflect the uniqueness and idioisyncracy of his or her account.

The date given at the start of each extract is the date the writing refers to, and not necessarily when it was written or published. For publication dates and further details please see the book list on p110.

'...not on horseback but on the shoulders of some honest Lancashire clown...'

LANDING

Walter Dixon Scott 1907

Liverpool is boldly different. She possesses, it seems, a singular faculty for moulding and co-ordinating. The peoples of the world pour through her streets, but they never interrupt her energetic introspectiveness. Fragments of this and that exotic race remain; they settle down, they breed, they pour their alien habits, their alien modes of thought, speech, religion, into the communal veins; but there is no perceptible change. The same emphatic lines of activity sweep on; the same special type is faithfully reproduced... Liverpool, it seems to me, is astonishingly self-absorbed. It is her own problems that chiefly interest her, and she has a habit of solving these problems for herself on self-invented lines. She has striven to work out – she is, as we shall see, still intently striving to work out – in ways of her own devising, the salvation of her proletariate. She has created a society that is quite untinged by the colours of the county. She has bred her local school of painters. Her politics are a strange sort of democratic conservatism. She is more civic than national, and the newspapers of this most cosmopolitan of English towns tend to reflect the movements of the City rather than the movements of the nation. And yet, she is not provincial. Manchester, her nearest neighbour, has her finely national *Guardian*, and touches the actual life of the metropolis with a far greater intimacy and frequency; and yet, of the two,

Manchester is clearly the more provincial. For provinciality, after all, is but a subordination to the metropolis, a reflection, half deliberate, half unconscious, of the life that goes on spontaneously at the centre. Well, Liverpool would be spontaneous, too. She will imitate no one, not even London. She will be her own metropolis. And those who have marked the clear efficiency of her designs, the unique mingling of American alertness and Lowland caution which colours the spirit that lives behind her very positive efforts, will admit that she has come bewilderingly near success.

Charles Dickens   1848

The best Hotel at Liverpool is one of the very best in England – the Adelphi. The Landlord, Mr Radley, is an excellent fellow, and much respected.

Allen Ginsberg   1965

I spent all week in Liverpool home of the Beatles and heard all the new rock bands and gave a little reading and had a ball with longhair boys – it's like San Francisco in Liverpool except the weather is greyer – lovely city, *mad* music, electronic hits your guts centers.

Paul Du Noyer   2002

Down by the Pier Head, at the foot of the Liver Building, the city sips at a river the colour of tea. At the landing stage the

Mersey Ferry boats bob, tenderly crushing fat tractor tyres slung from rusty chains. Evening will arrive any minute now and it will crown the whole scene with a huge tangerine sky. The cares of the day will be carried out to sea on a six-knot ebb-tide. Already you can hear a pub juke-box kick into life. Liverpool lights are coming on. And if the old are going home, the young are just getting started. The music is growing louder, and the first girl's shriek is about to pierce the misty air. This is a party town, and nothing gets in its way.

Libor Pesek   1987

When I first saw Liverpool it was a disrupted city. It reflected my soul. The city was in a shambles, my soul was in a shambles. We have much in common. Liverpudlians are emotional people and a loyal public. They helped us survive... After two concerts the orchestra proposed to me. I was 53 on the brink of old age. Funnily enough, I was; and this orchestra has made me young again.

Harriet Beecher Stowe   1853

About nine o'clock we were crossing the sand-bar, which lies at the mouth of the Mersey river, running up towards Liverpool. Our signal pennants are fluttering at the masthead, the pilot full of energy on one wheel-house, and a man casting the lead on the other.

'By the mark, five,' says the man. The pilot, with all his energy, is telegraphing to the steersman. It is a very close and complicated piece of navigation, I should think, this running up the Mersey, for every moment we are passing some kind of a signal-token, which warns off from some shoal. Here is a bell buoy, where the waves keep the bell always tolling; here, a buoyant lighthouse; and 'See there, those shoals, how pokerish they look!' says one of the passengers, pointing to the foam on our starboard bow. All is bustle, animation, exultation. Now float out the American stars and stripes on our bow.

Before us lies the great city of Liverpool. No old cathedral, no castles, a real New Yorkish place.

'There, that's the fort,' cries one. Bang, bang, go the two guns from our forward gangway.

'I wonder if they will fire from the fort,' says another.

'How green that grass looks!' says a third; 'and what pretty cottages!'

'All modern, though,' says somebody, in tones of disappointment. Now we are passing the Victoria Dock. Bang, bang, again. We are in a forest of ships of all nations; their masts bristling like the tall pines in Maine; their many-coloured flags streaming like the forest leaves in autumn.

'Hark,' says one; 'there's a chime of bells from the city; how sweet! I had quite forgotten it was Sunday.'

Here we cast anchor, and the small steam tender comes puffing alongside. Now for the custom-house officers. Staterooms, holds, and cabins must all give up their trunks; a general muster among the baggage, and passenger after passenger comes forward as their names are called, much as follows: 'Snooks.' 'Here sir.' 'Anything contraband here, Mr. Snooks? Any cigars, tobacco, &c.?' 'Nothing, sir.'

A little unlocking, a little fumbling. 'Shut up; all right; ticket here.' And a little man pastes on each article a slip of paper, with the royal arms of England and the magical letters V. R., to remind all men that they have come into a country where a lady reigns, and of course must behave themselves as prettily as they can.

We were inquiring of some friends for the most convenient hotel, when we found the son of Mr. Cropper, of Dingle Bank, waiting in the cabin, to take us with him to their hospitable abode. In a few moments after the baggage had been examined, we all  bade adieu to the old ship, and went on board the little steam tender, which carries passengers up to the city.

This Mersey river would be a very beautiful one, if it were not so dingy and muddy. As we are sailing up in the tender towards Liverpool, I deplore the circumstance feelingly. 'What does make this river so muddy?'

'O,' says a bystander, 'don't you know that "The quality of mercy is not strained"?'

Bishop James Jones   2003

Liverpool was the Heathrow of the 19th century.

Celia Fiennes   1698

I went to the ferry 9 miles to the River Meresy, another great river indeed much broader and a perfect sea for 20 mile or more; it comes out of Lancashire from Warrington and both this and the Dee empts themselves into the sea almost together a few leagues from Leverpoole which poole is form'd by a poynt of land that runs almost round the entrance from the sea, being narrow and hazardous to strangers to saile in in the winter, the mouth of the river by reason of the sands and rocks is a gate to the river; this I ferry'd over and was an hour and halfe in the passage, its of great bredth and at low water is so deep and salt as the sea almost, tho' it does not cast so green a hew on the water as the sea, but else the waves toss and the rocks great all round it and is as dangerous as the sea; its in a sort of Hoy that I ferried over and my horses, the boate would have held 100 people.

Leverpool which is in Lancashire is built just on the river Mersy, mostly new built houses of brick and stone after the London fashion; the first original was a few fishermens houses and now is grown to a large fine town and but a parish and one Church, tho' there be 24 streetes in it; there is indeed a little Chappell and there are a great many Dessenters in the town; its a very rich trading town the houses of brick and stone built high and even, that a streete quite through lookes very handsome, the streetes well pitched; there are abundance of persons you see very well dress'd and of good fashion; the streetes are faire and long, its London in miniature as much as ever I saw any thing; there is a very pretty Exchange stands on 8 pillars besides the corners which are each treble pillars all of stone and over which is a very handsome Town Hall; over all is a tower and cupillow thats so high that from thence one has the whole view of the town and the country round; in a clear day you may see the Isle of Man-which also was in view from out of Wales at Harding on the high tarrass walke in my Cos'n Percivalls garden.

Richard Acland Armstrong 1885

I came to Liverpool a stranger some six or seven years ago, knowing only that I was about to take up my residence in the second city of the mightiest Empire the world has ever seen. I admired its public buildings, its vast docks, its stately shipping, its splendid shops, its lovely parks. It seemed to me that this was a city in which one might be proud to be a citizen; a city which must be administered and governed by men of high capacity and generous temper.

But after the first glance I was appalled by one aspect of things here which pressed in upon my mind more and more for several weeks, till the pain of it became at times well nigh unbearable. The contiguity of immense wealth and abysmal poverty forced itself upon my notice. The hordes of the ragged and the wretched surged up from their native quarters and covered the noblest streets like a flood. Men and women in the cruellest grip of poverty, little children with shoeless feet, bodies pinched and faces in which the pure light of childhood had been quenched, swarmed on the very pavements that fronted the most brilliant shops; and the superb carriages of the rich, with their freights of refined and elegant ladies, threaded their way among sections of the population so miserable and squalid that my heart ached at the sight of them. I had seen wealth. I had seen poverty. But never before had I seen the two so jammed together.

Henry Brooks Adams   1858

The ocean, the *Persia*, Captain Judkins, and Mr G.P.R James, the most distinguished passenger, vanished one Sunday morning in a furious gale in the Mersey, to make place for the drearier picture of a Liverpool street as seen from the Adelphi coffee-room in November murk, followed instantly by the passionate delights of Chester and the romance of red-sandstone architecture. Millions of Americans have felt this succession of emotions. Possibly very young and ingenuous tourists feel them still, but in the days before tourists, when the romance was a reality, not a picture, they were overwhelming.

John Betjeman   1844

The 18th-century idea of a suburb was an extension of the town into the fields. A late and splendid example of this, which is too little regarded, is Birkenhead, where, beyond the Priory and the small village, a whole town of straight streets, broad squares and crescents enclosing a park, laid out by Paxton, was planned by two Scottish architects, Thomas Hamilton and Gillespie Graham, in 1844.

Hamilton Square is an impressive realisation of Hamilton's

scheme, and although many other streets of Birkenhead today lack the gracious buildings their architects intended, breadth and straightness survive. Birkenhead is probably the last example of a consciously planned town spreading over the fields in the 18th-century manner.

What we have come to think of as suburbs, alas in a faintly derogatory sense, is the opposite idea to what was in the heads of men like Hamilton in Birkenhead, Wood in Bath, Playfair in Edinburgh, Papworth in Cheltenham, Foulston in Plymouth. These were classical men who wanted to extend the town in to the country. The later suburb builder wanted to make country of towns.

John James Audubon   1826

When I landed it was raining. Yet the outward appearance of the city was agreeable. But no sooner had I entered it than the smoke from the coal fires was so oppressive on my lungs that I could scarcely breathe. I felt the same affecting my eyes also.

Robert Graves   1916

Officers of the Royal Welch were honorary members of the Formby Golf Club. Siegfried and I went there often. He played golf seriously, while I hit a ball alongside him. I had once played at Harlech as a junior member of the Royal St David's, but resigned when I found it bad for my temper. Afraid of taking the game up again seriously, I now limited myself to a single iron. My mis-hits did not matter. I played the fool and purposely put Siegfried off his game. This was a time of great food shortage; German submarines sank about every fourth food ship, and strict meat, butter, and sugar ration had been imposed. But the war had not reached the links. The leading Liverpool businessmen were members of the club, and did not mean to go short while there was any food at all coming in at the docks. Siegfried and I went to the club-house for lunch on the day before Christmas, and found a cold-buffet in the club dining-room, offering hams, barons of beef, jellied tongues, cold roast turkey, and chicken. A large, meaty-faced waiter presided. Siegfried asked him sarcastically: 'Is this all? There doesn't seem to be quite such a good spread as in previous years.' The waiter blushed. 'No, sir, this isn't quite up to the usual mark, sir, but we are expecting a more satisfactory consignment of meat on Boxing Day.' The dining-room at the club-house was always full, the links practically deserted.

Prince Albert 1846

It was always a cherished wish of mine to visit this scene of commerce, and all I have seen to-day has far surpassed my anticipations. The object of my visit here was a work of charity – a work reflecting the greatest credit on your liberality and good feeling, as it manifests that you are desirous of promoting the comfort of those who, by constant toil and labour, are contributing to the prosperity which I have seen this day.

George Stephenson 1827

My Dear,

Robert your very welcom letter dated Oct 26 1826 we duly received and was glad to here such good newes from Columbia respecting the mines but at the same time greatly disapointed at you not geting home so soon as was expected however I hope all will be for the best, and I must waddle on as well as I can until you get to joine me. There has been a florishing a count of your men in the English pappers and great creadit is given to Robert Stephenson for his good management of them. I must now let you know how we are getting on in this quarter. Yore mother is geting her tea beside me while I am riting this and in good spirits. she has been in Liverpool a bout a fortnight. we have got a very comfortable home, and a Roume set a side for Robert and Charels when they arive in England. We are getting raptily on with the tunnal under Liverpool it is 22 feet width & 16 feet high we have 6 shafts and driving right & left we have also got a great deal done on chat moss and on the same plans that I prepared befor parlament 2 years a go which plans was condemed by almost all the Engineers in England these plans is by cuting & imbanking with the moss some of the laths 12 feet high and stand remarkably well.

Lorenza Stevens Berbineau   1851

July 20th rainy this morning a Pilot came on board quite early we did not go into the Dock a steam Boat carried us to the warf it look very pretty when we came in sight of Liverpool we arrived there about 2 Oclo we got into a carriage went to the Adelphi Hotel, kept by James Radley. the sides of the streets are paved & the centre is Mackadamized the cross walks are flag stone Mr Putnam & Mr Allen & Mrs Snodgrass families came to the Hotel were we are we took clothing in Carpet bags for the night the Custom House officers came on Board examined what things we took. we dined to day at five Oclock I have just came in from a walk One of my fellow passengers went with me Miss Clink we saw several fine buildings we walk in St James Cemetry fine looking place we took tea half past eight. the room Edie & I have nice room a mahogany bedsted the posts are as high as the ceiling with red damask wosted curtains and the same at the windows.

Margaret Cole

At the beginning of 1910 my father accepted the Professorship of Latin at Liverpool, a job which was near to pioneering, for the University was inclined to regard the arts as frills compared with serious subjects such as naval architecture, in which it was pre-eminent, and he had an uphill fight to obtain adequate recognition. We children were parked in various places while the furniture went on its laborious way by goods train, and on a cold damp January day found ourselves in a large four-storied house in Princes Park Terrace near Sefton Park.

I had already been two years at boarding-school when we moved, and Liverpool never took the place of Cambridge in my heart. I have a certain mild affection for it, sufficient to feel sorry when I heard that it had taken a week's heavy pasting in the spring of '41, when the Luftwaffe was trying to knock out the harbours of Britain; but that feeling does not go deep, and I have never been back to it since, on my father's retirement, my family returned to Cambridge after ten years' exile. I do not think any of us liked it very much; we were Easterlings to the core, and never got on terms with the grey dampness of Lancashire, the dirt and the harsh voices. You were warned not to keep your clothes shut up too long in wardrobes, in case they mildewed, but to put them out in the sun – only there never seemed to be any sun! There is, it is true, a sea-wind from the Mersey, strong enough at times to blow small children off their feet, which dissipates the smoke from the Widnes soap and chemical works and other factories, and prevents the grimy fog which overhangs Manchester from lying so long in Liverpool; but in compensation the salt in the air seemed to induce the particles of carbon to coagulate in lumps. I have never seen such *enormous* smuts as there were in Liverpool; you could watch them drifting towards you, and dodge them if you could; if you failed they spilt themselves down your nose. That same smoke, however, produced a murky beauty which was not to be found in Cambridge, lurid red and purple sunsets which we could see from the top windows of the house in Princes Park when the sun went down behind the dark line of the Clwyddian mountains on the far side of Dee. We were told by patriotic Liverpudlians that Turner practised his sunsets on Merseyside.

Liverpool introduced us, also, to ships and mountains. We were not encouraged to roam about the dock area, which was dirty and supposed to be full of dangerous characters; the dock population was in fact mixed and pretty rowdy. But anyone could take a tram – if you had the little ones with you, a first-class tram – to Pier Head, and watch the liners come in and the tenders fussing to and fro between the landing-stage and the big Cunarders, the *Lusitania* and the *Mauretania*, which even then were too big to stay alongside, but lay to the south in the wide and deep Sloyne opposite Garston. You could take one of the ferry-boats to Birkenhead or Port Sunlight or New Brighton, and walk across the Wirral peninsula to the Sands of Dee, or round it past Hoylake golf-course looking to see what jetsam the sea had thrown up. Wrecks played a distinct part in the economy of Liverpool. I remember picking up quantities of onions and oranges which had come ashore from a Spanish boat; the mammoth stores like Owen Owen's were constantly announcing 'salvage sales' (from fire as well as water), and once the wreck of a ship full of paint caused great pieces of the city to appear in new coats of a peculiarly ugly bluish-green.

Washington Irving

It was a fine sunny morning when the thrilling cry of 'land!' was given from the mast-head. None but those who have experienced it can form an idea of the delicious throng of sensations which rush into an American's bosom, when he first comes in sight of Europe. There is a volume of associations with the very name. It is the land of promise, teeming with everything of which his childhood has heard, or on which his studious years have pondered.

From that time, until the moment of arrival, it was all fever-ish excitement. The ships of war, that prowled like guardian giants along the coast; the headlands of Ireland, stretching out into the channel; the Welsh mountains towering into the clouds; -- all were objects of intense interest. As we sailed up the Mersey, I reconnoitred the shores with a telescope. My eye dwelt with delight on neat cottages, with their trim shrub-beries and green grass-plots. I saw the mouldering ruin of an abbey overrun with ivy, and the taper spire of a village church rising from the brow of a neighboring hill; – all were characteristic of England.

The tide and wind were so favorable, that the ship was enabled to come at once to her pier. It was thronged with people; some idle lookers-on; others, eager expectants of friends or relations. I could distinguish the merchant to whom the ship was consigned. I knew him by his calculating brow and restless air. His hands were thrust into his pockets; he was whistling thoughtfully, and walking to and fro, a small space having been accorded him by the crowd, in deference to his temporary importance. There were repeated cheerings and salutations interchanged between the shore and the ship, as friends happened to recognize each other. I particularly noticed one young woman of humble dress, but interesting demeanor. She was leaning forward from among the crowd; her eye hurried over the ship as it neared the shore, to catch some wished-for countenance. She seemed disappointed and sad; when I heard a faint voice call her name. – It was from a poor sailor who had been ill all the voyage, and had excited the sympathy of every one on board. When the weather was fine, his messmates had spread a mattress for him on deck in the shade, but of late his illness had so increased that he had taken to his hammock, and only breathed a wish that he might see his wife before he died. He had been helped on deck as we came up the river, and was now leaning against the shrouds, with a countenance so wasted, so pale, so ghastly, that it was no wonder even the eye of affection did not recognize him. But at the sound of his voice, her eye darted on his features: it read, at once, a whole volume of sorrow; she clasped her hands, uttered a faint shriek, and stood wringing them in silent agony.

All now was hurry and bustle. The meetings of acquaintances – the greetings of friends – the consultations of men of business. I alone was solitary and idle. I had no friend to meet, no cheering to receive. I stepped upon the land of my forefathers – but felt that I was a stranger in the land.

Henry Booth   1827

During the whole of the year 1827, the formation of the Tunnel under Liverpool was carried forward with spirit and perseverance. Night and day the excavation proceeded, and many difficulties in the execution of the work had to be overcome. In some places the substance excavated was a soft blue shale, with abundance of water; in other places a wet sand presented itself, requiring no slight labour and contrivance to support till the masonry which was to form the roof was erected. In passing under Crown-street, near the Botanic Garden, for want of sufficient props the superincumbent mass fell in from the surface, being a depth of 30 feet, of loose moss-earth and sand. On some occasions the miners refused to work, and it not unfrequently required the personal superintendence and encouragement of the Engineer to keep them at their posts. Nor is this surprising, considering the nature of the operation: boring their way almost in the dark, with the water streaming around them, and uncertain whether the props and stays would bear the pressure from above till the arch-work should be completed. Those who visit the Tunnel in its present state, illuminated with gas-lights, and traversed by horses, carriages, and crowds of passengers, will not easily picture to themselves the original dark and dangerous cavern, with the roof and sides supported by shores, while the miners pursued their arduous task by the light of a few candles, whose feeble glimmer glancing on the water which ran down the sides, or which spread out in a sheet below, was barely sufficient to show the dreariness of the place.

Neil Cossons 2003

Liverpool is beyond question one of the great cities of the world. Twenty-first century Liverpool is undergoing an extraordinary period of development that will change the way Liverpool looks for ever.

Karel Capek 1924

Of course, I had a look at the harbours and I saw so many of them that now I mix them up. Well, wait a bit, Folkestone, London, Leith, Glasgow – that's four; then Liverpool, Bristol, Plymouth, and possibly there are others.....

But Liverpool, reader, Liverpool is the biggest; and for its size I now pardon it for the harm it did me. Owing to some congress or royal visitor or whatever it was, it would not grant the wayfarer a night's lodging; and it terrified me with a new cathedral, big and hopeless like the ruins of the baths of Caracallus at Rome. And at midnight it enveloped itself in a Puritanic darkness to prevent me from finding my way to a wretched inn, which gave me a bed as damp and sour-smelling as a tub of cabbage – well, as I say, I forgive Liverpool all this, for there was something worth seeing from Dingle to Bootle and still further to Birkenhead on the other side – yellow water, puffing steam ferries, tug-boats, like pot-bellied, black hogs rocking on the waves, white Atlantic liners, docks, basins, towers, cranes, silos, elevators, smoking factories, stevedores, barks, warehouses, wharves, casks, packing-cases, tubs, bales, chimneys, masts, rigging, trains, smoke, chaos, yelling, clanging, clattering, panting, rent bellies of ships, smell of horses, of sweat, of foul water and garbage from all parts of the earth; and if I were to go on heaping up words for another half hour I should not prove a match for that sum-total of quantity, confusion and extent which is called Liverpool. Beautiful is the steamer when with a screech it scatters the water with its broad breast, hurling smoke from its stout funnels; it is beautiful when it vanishes beyond the arched shoulder of the waters, dragging a veil of smoke behind it. Beautiful is the distance and the goal, O man, you who stand on the bow as you depart. Beautiful is the sailing-boat which glides over the waves, beautiful is departure and arrival. My sealess country, is not your horizon somewhat narrow, and do you not lack the murmur of distant places? Yes, yes, but there can be bustle of expanses around our heads; even if we cannot navigate, we can at least indulge in thought, furrow on wings of the spirit the broad and high world; I tell you, there is still room enough for expeditions and for big ships. Yes, it is needful to keep on sailing forth; the ocean is in all places where courage is.

But, steersman, I beg of you, do not turn back; we are not yet sailing home. Let us linger here in this roadstead of Liverpool and look at everything before we return; it is vast, dirty and noisy. Where is the real England, I wonder? There in those quiet and clean cottages amid the fearfully ancient trees and traditions, in the homes of people who are in the pitch of perfection, peaceable and refined, or here on these turbid waves, in the clattering docks, in Manchester, Poplar, Glasgow's Broomielaw? Well, I must confess that I do not understand this; there in that England almost too much perfection and beauty; and here, here almost too much...

Well, I do not understand it; it is not like the same country and the same people. So be it, let us sail forth; let the ocean splash me, let the wind buffet me; I think that I have seen too much.

Joseph Ballard   1815

At our landing on the wharf at Liverpool we were surrounded by a tribe of girls of the town who welcomed us most cheerfully.

These and innumerable others whom we met in going to our lodgings, together with the sombre appearance of the buildings, first by lamplight made visible, gave me no favorable opinion of the place. After a long walk which (owing to inactivity on board ship) fatigued me exceedingly I arrived at the Liverpool Arms (the Inn where Silliman lodged and whose waiter Louis he had most unjustly accused of practising by his politeness upon the purses of the customers). The appearance of the attendants at an inn with hair bepowdered and dressed in an appropriate style was to me so new that it was some time before I could make up resolution to call in a consequential tone to the waiter to bring me anything wanted.

James Chadwick 1941

We had quite a lot of bombing raids. Practically all the windows in my laboratory were blown out...fortunately very little damage was caused. The cyclotron was partly below ground – it was in the basement... For about a week they were blown in every night, and we put up cardboard shutters. Every night they would be blown in again. We'd just put them up in the morning and go on.

The Builder 1865

It is this mixture of wealth with penury that is another distinctive feature in Liverpool. In the metropolis a fine site is usually occupied with houses of corresponding and nearly uniform appearance. But the Trafalgar-square of Liverpool, though having many points in common with that of London, has a strong dash of Tottenham-court-road thrown into it, by the existence of a few shabby unworthy houses among the buildings surrounding it. Standing under the terraced portico of the Free Library, and looking upon St. George's Hall and the railway station, as one might look upon St. Martin's church and Northumberland House from the entrance to the National Gallery, the resemblance of the two sites is striking, even to the street opening out of it in a similar position to that occupied by Parliament-street. But here the resemblance ceases. The houses in this street are small and dirty, and should make way for better ones. Their chimney-pots occupy the position that should be occupied by the drawing-room floors of a handsome class of buildings. Although one side of the square is sumptuous with the enormous American hotel, another side has an ugly eyesore in a shabby group composed of an American and Canadian kerosine and petroleum oil depôt, a cigar-shop, a frail bazaar, an eating-house, the turning into a narrow dingy street, called Livesleyplace, two or three old public-houses, – the Warriors' Rest and the Angel to wit, and Bentley's book-store, most of which, specimens of the domestic and commercial architecture of the last age, are made still more garish by enormous announcements of the wares dealt in by their proprietors permanently painted upon them in huge black letters.

A few masterly touches, such as the removal of inadequate objects occupying conspicuous sites, and Liverpool would be more like the cities of the ancient classic world than anything we have.

Bryan Blundell   1707

20 March

We got to Liverpool, all things well with us. I bless the Lord for all his great mercies to us. We had little damage to the ship. After discharge, had the ship on shore drove all new trunnels in her bottom and sheathed her, made her very strong. Put 26 guns in her and fitted her for fight by good close quarters and all things necessary, which, with fitting out for the voyage, cost us £1,400. She made £1,750 freight for us from Virginia.

Staying long at home, and my former wife being dead near four years, I thought it time to take another, so married Elizabeth Lively, oldest daughter of John Lievesly.

Herman Melville   1839

After running till about midnight, we 'hove-to' near the mouth of the Mersey; and next morning, before day-break, took the first of the flood; and with a fair wind, stood into the river; which, at its mouth, is quite an arm of the sea. Presently, in the misty twilight, we passed immense buoys, and caught sight of distant objects on shore, vague and shadowy shapes, like Ossian's ghosts.

As I stood leaning over the side, and trying to summon up some image of Liverpool, to see how the reality would answer to my conceit; and while the fog, and mist, and gray dawn were investing every thing with a mysterious interest, I was startled by the doleful, dismal sound of a great bell, whose slow intermitting tolling seemed in unison with the solemn roll of the billows. I thought I had never heard so boding a sound; a sound that seemed to speak of judgment and the resurrection, like belfry-mouthed Paul of Tarsus.

It was not in the direction of the shore; but seemed to come out of the vaults of the sea, and out of the mist and fog.

Who was dead, and what could it be?

I soon learned from my shipmates, that this was the famous *Bell-Buoy*, which is precisely what its name implies; and tolls fast or slow, according to the agitation of the waves. In a calm, it is dumb; in a moderate breeze, it tolls gently; but in a gale, it is an alarum like the tocsin, warning all mariners to flee. But it seemed fuller of dirges for the past, than of monitions for the future; and no one can give ear to it, without thinking of the sailors who sleep far beneath it at the bottom of the deep.

Captain Greenvile Collins   1687

Being on the back of Hylesand, bring the Mill and Wood one on the other, as in the Chart, Number 30. and run in keeping close alongst Hylesand, and so into Highlake, and Anchor. Here the great ships that belong to Liverpool put out part of their Lading till the Ships are light enough to sail over the Flats to Liverpool. There is a Channel near Formby to go into Liverpool, where there is three Fathom at low-water on the Bar; but this place is not Buoy'd nor Bekon'd, and so not known: the Ships lye aground before the Town of Liverpool;

'tis bad riding afloat before the Town, by reason of the strong Tydes that run here; therefore Ships that ride afloat, ride up at the Sleyne where is less tyde.

Agnes Cowper 1905

It was in June, 1905, and I was on holiday with a girl friend, spending the week in daily excursions to places of local interest. It was my friend who suggested a visit to Port Sunlight, and as I had never been there I gladly agreed to her proposal. Upon arrival I was astonished to find a village of great beauty, with wide open spaces, tree-lined avenues containing rows of pretty cottages each differing in style of architecture and replete with many amenities to cheer and help its inhabitants. It appeared strange, and, indeed, almost unbelievable to find that all this was posssible instead of the dismal surroundings, narrow streets and general drabness which at that time was accepted as the inevitable environment of factory life as developed in Lancashire and elsewhere. A tour through the spacious offices and model factory, with its large, clean, and airy departments induced in me an ardent wish to exchange my back-room office in a depressing part of central Liverpool for employment in these beautiful surroundings. The offices looked so imposing that, for a moment, I stood aghast at my own audacity in imagining that I could qualify for a position that would enable this desire to be fulfilled. At school, as a child, I must have assimilated the precept which, at the head of my copy-book commended me, in the event of my not at first succeeding, to try, try, try again, for, after obeying this injunction in a series of applications for a place on the staff of Messrs. Lever Brothers Limited, my efforts were finally successful, for on the 13th February, 1906, I was appointed to a position, albeit a modest one, in the Head Office, then at Port Sunlight. My friends thought me foolish to give up employment in Liverpool for a berth which would necessitate a long tram-boat-foot journey, especially as my commencing salary would be no higher, save for free tickets for the Mersey ferry service. But I would not take their advice. Hitherto circumstance had compelled me to accept any post I could secure, but now, freed from certain duties to the home, I was determined to exercise my own judgement.

For the first two years my work required me to be in attendance at 8 a.m., but after that period, at 8-30 a.m. Each morning, on reaching the Liverpool Pier Head in time to board the 7-15 steamer to New Ferry, I experienced a pleasurable sense of adventure. In summer it was delightful to walk the deck with a congenial companion whose destination was also mine, and, in the freshness of the early morning, to meet that swelling tide with its tang of the sea breathing the varied maritime interests which serve to ennoble the Mersey. And in winter, to gather in the warm saloon, there to be tossed about by the strength of a heavy gale; then to land at New Ferry and struggle up the long pier in the teeth of a strong sou'-wester, a stimulus which produced a feeling of exhilaration, and provided a tonic for the demands of the day. My work was interesting and although we were subject to strict but not severe discipline, we were free from irksome restraint and petty control. Each had his or her particular tasks and if these were discharged satisfactorily work proceeded with a freedom which stimulated all to give of their best.

Samuel Sullivan Cox 1851

Here we are upon substantial soil. Liverpool! How languidly the word melts in the mouth! My partiality for steamships and big ponds could not restrain the outbreak of joy with which we pressed the solid land. The effects too of our experience, though sad at first; have resulted in a bound of animal spirits almost inconsistent with sanity.

At the mouth of the Mersey we took a pilot aboard, and with our 'starboard, sir,' 'port, sir,' and 'steady, sir,' we reached Liverpool at 11 o'clock, upon the night of the 17th of May, 1851. It was some recompense for missing the green, bright green banks of the Mersey, with its cottages and residences, that we passed up amid a galaxy of many-colored lights, which, reflected upon the water from Birkenhead on the one side, and Liverpool on the other, almost transformed the scene into one of fairyland. Our guns boomed; mails were taken; and after the custom-house proceedings, by no means vexatious, we were permitted to land. The first person that spoke to me was a little imp, modelled after the exterior of Oliver Twist. A police officer touched him with a bâton. He was *non est* in a jiffy.

Our first impression of the population here was not very favorable. True, we saw the fag-end of humanity in the shape of beggars and loafers at the landing. We had no sooner taken up our march to our hotel, preferring to feel the delight of a walk, after so long a ride on the billows, than a fellow who said that he was a servant at the Waterloo, offered himself as our pilot. I suspected him, but thought that we would use him, as it was nearly two in the morning. We had not gone far before we were saluted with, 'Which hotel, sir – which hotel?'

'Waterloo!'

'Sorry-very sorry-can't accommodate you, sir-I'm boots at the Waterloo, sir-all full, sir. Three ship-loads just arrived, sir-very sorry-Victoria Hotel near by-few minutes walk, sir-own sister of the Waterloo keeps it.'

He had said too much. We marched on, heartily laughing at 'Boots!' Saint Somebody's church illuminated the hour of two, and it was nearly daylight – a phenomenon belonging to this northern clime which considerably bewildered our Buckeye experience. We found the Waterloo open, and the lady at the door with her servants, ready to take down our names. I introduced our pilot as their servant. They, of course, disclaimed his acquaintance. 'You are a pretty specimen of human veracity.'

'Yes, sir, I am obliged to you, sir.'

'But I suppose we ought to pay you for your guidance?'

'Oh yes, please you, sir, you are very kind, sir.'

I gave him a shilling, with a caution about lying, which he, with a rub over his red nose, and a low bow, acknowledged.

We had scarcely appeared this morning at our window, when that extreme of English civilization called 'starvation' was seen in the shape of a young urchin, whether boy or girl I could not discern; for the dress consisted of only two rags. He stood bobbing his head and whining, while I sketched him. His counterfeit presentment followed us, as soon as we left the hotel to take a stroll; and the little gipsey had the same monotone of grief. He was joined by another, and thus marshalled, we had to pass the agony of some squares. It was not until a fretful threat to 'cut his weazand,' that he cut our company, which he did with the remark, 'they won't pay any more.'

How comfortably every thing is conducted in these English hotels. We have our own parlors, and our own meals. It looks so cosey to see our own good company presiding at the tea-urn, and dispensing the Johnsonian beverage.

Edward Chambré Hardman 1950

In those days we were living at Barnston, in Wirral and we used to come to town every day by car, and pass the end of Holt Hill. Now, to begin with, the *Ark Royal* was very hard to see, it was painted with greys and browns and all sorts of camouflage paints, and gradually they got her painted up in readiness for the visit of the Queen Mother to perform the opening ceremony. So the camouflage gradually went and instead they gave her this white undercoat, and then she looked wonderful riding over all these houses and all the smoke and muck of Merseyside, in fact the muck of Merseyside was one of the things which made the subject attractive because without that she wouldn't have stood out like she does here. And having decided that that was a worthwhile subject, I had to look around for possible vantage spots.

I wondered about a high viewpoint to show more of the roadway further down and eventually I plumped for the actual top of Holt Hill, waiting for the sun to be right and so on. And me with my camera set up on a tripod here. This little boy appeared and of course he was too near the camera to begin with, so I let him go on a bit hoping that he wouldn't go on too far and I just got him at that spot. He looks like a schoolboy but he may be selling newspapers or delivering newspapers, something of the sort. Anyway, that was the place to get him.

Michael Howard   2004

I cut my political teeth in Liverpool and have long had great admiration and affection for its people.

Geoff Davies   1961

It was one of the most exciting things I've seen in my life. The first time I came across them was at an all-night jazz session, and we were horrified to find what we considered a pop band getting in on it. So we got a pass-out at the door to go down the pie stall at the Pier Head. I remember them starting up as we went out and I thought, What a fucking racket.

But the following week I went to a lunchtime session and there were the Beatles again. And that was it, everything changed for me. They used to do 'Money' and extend the intro, really bloody heavy, and then Lennon comes in: 'The best things in life are free', in the dirtiest, foulest voice I'd heard in my life, full of hate and sneering and cynicism. I couldn't believe the anarchy. The cheek of them....

Malcolm Lowry   1928

How strange the landing at Liverpool, the Liver Building seen
once more through the misty rain, that murk smelling already
of nosebags and Caegwyrle Ale – the familiar deep-draughted
cargo steamers, harmoniously masted, still sternly sailing
outward bound with the tide, worlds of iron hiding their
crews from the weeping black-shawled women on the piers.

Liverpool Courier   1909

Many thousands of people yesterday afternoon and evening
availed themselves of the opportunity afforded by the
proprietors, Messrs. F. W. Woolworth & Co. Ltd., of inspect-
ing their new stores at Church Street and Williamson Street.
The handsome premises, formerly occupied by Henry Miles
& Co., were thronged the whole time they were open, many
no doubt attracted by the novel character of the business

 transacted. 6D is the highest price
charged for any single article in the
establishment, but the variety of
articles obtainable is infinite. Though
none were on sale, the goods were
laid out ready for the commencement
of business to-day, and occasioned
the visitors considerable surprise in
the matter of their exceptional value.
Two orchestras were engaged in discoursing music yesterday,
and there was a constant run on the tea room where the
proprietors supplied free teas to all who were fortunate
enough to reach the room through the crush.

Daniel Defoe   c1720

I entered Lancashire at the remotest western point of that county, having been at West-Chester upon a particular occasion, and from thence ferried over from the Cestrian Chersonesus, as I have already called it, to Liverpoole. This narrow slip of land, rich, fertile and full of inhabitants, though formerly, as authors say, a mere waste and desolate forest, is called Wirall or by some Wirehall. Here is a ferry over the Mersee, which, at full sea, is more than two miles over. We land on the flat shore on the other side, and are contented to ride through the water for some length, not on horseback but on the shoulders of some honest Lancashire clown, who comes knee deep to the best side, to truss you up, and then runs away with you, as nimbly as you desire to ride, unless his trot were easier; for I was shaken by him that I had the luck to be carried by more than I cared for, and much worse than a hard trotting horse would have shaken me.

William Wells Brown   1849

At a little past three o'clock, the ship cast anchor, and we were tumbled, bag and baggage, into a small steamer, and in a few moments were at the door of the Custom-House. The passage had only been nine days and twenty-two hours, the quickest on record at that time, yet it was long enough. I waited nearly three hours before my name was called, and when it was, I unlocked my trunks and handed them over to one of the officers, whose dirty hands made no improvement on the work of the laundress. First one article was taken out, and then another, till an Iron Collar that had been worn by a female slave on the banks of the Mississippi, was hauled out, and this democratic instrument of torture became the centre of attraction; so much so, that instead of going on with the examination, all hands stopped to look at the 'Negro Collar.'

Several of my countrymen who were standing by, were not a little displeased at answers which I gave to questions on the subject of Slavery; but they held their peace. The interest created by the appearance of the Iron Collar, closed the examination of my luggage. As if afraid that they would find something more hideous, they put the Custom-House mark on each piece, and passed them out, and I was soon comfortably installed at Brown's Temperance Hotel, Clayton Square.

No person of my complexion can visit this country without being struck with the marked difference between the English and the Americans. The prejudice which I have experienced on all and every occasion in the United States, and to some extent on board the Canada, vanished as soon as I set foot on the soil of Britain.

Dr William Henry Duncan   1843

The disease I refer to is FEVER, – the common fever of this country, which may be taken as a generic term, including the varieties known as typhus, synochus, low adynamic fever, brain fever, nervous fever, &c., and which I shall presently show to be the characteristic disease of the poor of Liverpool. With regard to one, at least, of the conditions noticed, i.e. the congregation of the inhabitants within small and pent-up areas, where the means of ventilation are denied, (and where, as I formerly observed, the atmosphere is vitiated not by their respiration only, but by the poisonous emanations which arise from their bodies), there can be little doubt as to its being an efficient cause of fever, the fact being established by the concurrent testimony of nearly every medical writer of repute. The operation of this cause, in its highest intensity, is shewn in the case of the Black Hole of Calcutta, where, out of 146 human beings who were confined within a space of about 5000 cubic feet, not more than twenty-three survived the night, and these 'were said to have been afterwards attacked with a fever analogous to typhus.' The same cause acting in a less concentrated form, produces the same effects, more slowly, it is true, but not the less surely, in the 'black holes,' – the crowded courts, and cellars, and lodging-houses, with which Liverpool abounds.

John Lennon   1964

Reviving the old tradition of Judro Bathing is slowly but slowly dancing in Liddypool once more. Had you remembering these owld custard of Boldy Street blowing? The Peer Hat is very popularce for sun eating and Boots for Nude Brighter is handys when sailing. We are not happy with her Queen Victorious Monologue, but Walky Through Gallery is goodly when the rain and Sit Georgic House is black (and white from the little pilgrims flying from Hellsy College). Talk Hall is very histerical with old things wot are fakes and King Anne never slept there I tell you. Shout Airborne is handly for planes if you like (no longer government patrolled) and the L.C.C.C. (Liddypool Cha Cha Cha) are doing a great thing. The Mersey Boat is selling another three copies to some go home foreigners who went home.

There is a lot to do in Liddypool, but not all convenience.

Margaret Fuller 1846

At the first sight of the famous Liverpool Docks, extending miles on each side of our landing, we felt ourselves in a slower, solider, and not on that account less truly active, state of things than at home. That impression is confirmed. There is not as we travel that rushing, tearing, and swearing, that snatching of baggage, that prodigality of shoe-leather and lungs, which attend the course of the traveller in the United States; but we do not lose our 'goods,' we do not miss our car. The dinner, if ordered in time, is cooked properly, and served punctually, and at the end of the day more that is permanent seems to have come of it than on the full-drive system. But more of this, and with a better grace, at a later day.

Samuel Derrick 1760

There are at Leverpoole three good inns. For ten-pence a man dines elegantly at an ordinary consisting of ten or a dozen dishes. Indeed, it must be said, both of Cheshire and Lancashire, that they have plenty of the best and most luxurious foods at a very cheap rate: their mutton is small and juicy; their fowl, whether wild or tame, brought in fine order to market; and of fish they have great variety in the utmost perfection.

Hugh Shimmin 1860

There are few sights in Liverpool which are more surprising and gratifying to a stranger than the magnificent Landing Stages, at the George's and Prince's Piers. Indeed, to many 'natives,' these structures are a source of healthy and invigorating enjoyment; and thousands daily use them as such. In the nature of things this was to be expected. Hundreds of people whose business or means compel them to live in the more densely populated parts of the town, make a daily practice of taking a walk to enjoy the sea breeze and fresh air on our Landing Stages. What the Parks are to some towns, the Landing Stages are to Liverpool.

It is not to be wondered at, seeing the vast and teeming population which surround us, that the enjoyment of such a privilege as a walk on the Landing Stages afford, should be greatly abused. The fact of the public being allowed to use it without let or hindrance has caused this abuse; and the scenes witnessed here, on Sunday evenings more particularly, have long been a reproach to the local authorities. Still, on this as on all other matters which exhibit moral or social degradation, there exists a difference of opinion. This difference is caused in the main by a misapprehension of the facts. People who have not seen the Landing Stages on a Sunday evening, will not believe that the evil has reached that magnitude as to warrant its being publicly noticed in the Council.

The crowded state of the small Landing Stage on Sunday evenings cannot have escaped the most casual observer. It is a busy day with the Ferries. The pent-up artizan rejoices, and often indulges, in the Sunday trip to Cheshire; and an increase of several thousand passengers to and fro will, as a matter of course, affect the gathering on the Stage. But those who cross the river, for purposes of recreation, are not those who crowd the Stage, and call forth public indignation. No.

Young lads and girls who began by going there for a walk, soon made it a meeting-place. Older heads, with more vicious intentions, then began to frequent the stage, and it has gone on from bad to worse, until now it is almost impossible for a female to pass to or from the Ferries without being subjected to the rudeness, vulgarity, obscenity, or profanity of the shameless hordes, of both sexes, who congregate on, and pollute the stage by their presence.

The girls who frequent the stage, and by their gaudy dress, rude speeches, and unseemly conduct, excite the disgust of all well disposed people, are not such as have given themselves up wholly to a dissolute life. They are not 'social evils' proper. The majority of them are engaged in some industrial occupation during the week, and this is their mode of enjoyment on the Sabbath. They here meet with young men, and the promenading of these groups, mingled with the jeers, laughter, and filthy conversation, is what constitutes the great public nuisance so justly complained of.

'Fast young men' were not long in scenting out what they term 'the game of the Landing Stage.' It is with no simple or virtuous intention that you see the 'pork-pie' and the 'turn-down' bearing away to the Landing Stage, on Sunday evening. After meeting a girl here for two or three evenings in succession, and perhaps meeting her at a dancing class during the week, it is found easy to persuade her to accompany them to Eastham or Bidston, and in five cases which have been painfully brought under notice, the girls' ruin had been effected by these young scoundrels and by such means. Parents are now mourning the loss of daughters, and girls are now outcasts on the streets; and these fearful results can be traced to the permitted indecency and immorality on the Landing Stage.

But it is not the 'lower orders,' as some people term it, that are solely to blame for the disgraceful scenes. It is not the 'fast young men' either. The evil would never have reached such a magnitude had it not received more substantial support. On a Sunday evening recently, we noticed men of good position, (one of whom had filled public offices in this town, and had a wife and family at home,) leering and chatting with girls, whom they would in daylight, or in the public streets, be ashamed to acknowledge. There was noticed also one of our great public men who lives at this side of the water, landing from the Rock Ferry boat. He appeared to have been wooing the rosy god, or in plainer terms, he was partially intoxicated. He stood a little time by the south refreshment room, gnawing the head of his cane and reeling about now and then, noticing the while the girls that passed, and occasionally tapping some of them on the shoulder or hat. Having completed his resolve, he joined a group, and in a few minutes after was seen talking to a very young girl – a child, or little more – and by the eight o'clock boat this couple crossed to Seacombe.

There were several of the young girls there under the influence of drink, and the gross indecency of their language was inexpressibly vile. The young men in their company seemed to be quite their equals, so far as foulness of speech and riotous behaviour were concerned; but the number of aged men, of decent exterior, who promenaded and seemed to enjoy the scene, was the most suggestive sight. To think of men who will walk to Church with their daughters in the morning, spend the afternoon with their amiable families, and yet devote the evening of the sacred day to the encouragement of such abominable profanity.

It sounds well at public meetings to hear men talking of taking 'a deep interest in all that concerns the people's happiness.' It is easy to condemn the conduct of the lower classes; but there is nothing that encourages immorality so much, or corrupts the manners of the lower classes more, than the looseness, the vicious indulgence, and the filthy hypocrisy of 'well-to-do people.' By their conduct they foster, feed and perpetuate all manner of evils, and were it not for them, brothels would not be so numerous, neither would the Landing Stage be such a great public scandal.

Edinburgh Review   1811

On the first of the present month of August, 1811, a vessel
arrived at Liverpool, with a cargo from Sierra Leone, the
owner, master, mate, and whole crew of which are free
Negroes. The master, who is also owner, is the son of an
American Slave, and is said to be very well skilled both in
trade and navigation, as well as to be of a very pious and
moral character. It must have been a strange and animating
spectacle to see this free and enlightened African entering, as
an independent trader, with his black crew, into that port
which was so lately the nidus of the Slave Trade.

Frederick Gibberd   1967

The two towers now react on the Liverpool scene and on each
other in the most diverse and often surprising ways: they can
be balanced; more often one dominates the other; but at all
times one is conscious that Liverpool has two crowns of equal
prominence.

Niall Griffiths   1915

And still beyond that the sea at Prestatyn and the River Dee
which must be traversed by ferry above the mud at low tide
black and reeking or indeed skirted at Chester this route in
fact taken by the train to the Birkenhead docks where
warships appeared in the water beneath the tall and claw-
fingered cranes facing the other docks across the murky
Mersey where also other vessels would appear, those outgo-
ing filled with singing and a celebration of sorts and those
returning drifting silently into dock themselves like

phantoms, these huge ships cargoed with pain and loss, and floating across the gangplanks those who have left their limbs and more commonly their minds elsewhere. Then across the conurbation the bricks and cobbles and human mass, that huddled hysteria that characterises port cities and what might Katie find there in that storm of mingled life?

John Hamilton 1984

We got to the point, when the Thatcher government got in – the Callaghan government lost – and she started putting the pressure on with the Rate Support Grant. You can manipulate the Rate Support Grant quite easily, Labour had done it but she did it with a vengeance. So that the cities or towns in the south of England like Brighton and Eastbourne and so on, were actually floating in money, whereas we had been cut in order to balance them out. The result was of course, in the industrial north we were having to put rates up and cut our services. Of course the general public doesn't see all that, and see the mechanics of the whole thing, and of course we were getting the blame for poor services with high rates.

It came the year when they cut £30 million off us in the Rate Support Grant and that was the particular year when they were offering us a Garden Festival site and the cost of that, which the government would pay for, was £30 million. So they were shifting it from one pocket to another. They were getting the credit for the Garden Festival, which they were taking off our money which we needed for basic services and so on, and again we were in the situation of Liverpool, the last in the queue as it were, still standing there by our faith, and that. And we went right to the bitter end and got expelled from the Council by the High Court.

I always remember Lord Woolf who tried us with the Lord High Justice, you know the Lord Chief Justice at the present moment, saying that 'it didn't matter how much the people needed the money, it didn't matter whether they'd lost their homes or not, it didn't matter whether they were hungry or not, our job is not to go bankrupt, not to exceed more than you're entitled to and you've got to let people go unemployed, and to go without houses – that's not your worry – you have to obey the law and let those people suffer'.

An awful lot of people in the Labour group, like myself, who had no thought about Militant as such, just didn't like the whole situation we were in and we were prepared to stand up to it. You might as well say that Sylvia Pankhurst was a militant because she was demanding votes for women. Every sort of step forward in political life has been a 'militancy' that has done it, in a sense, and I put the word 'militancy' in inverted commas. It's not really a militancy, it's really a sort of social feeling.

Mrs Thatcher experienced that, bear in mind that we came in on the Council here, in that period where we came very near to getting the majority at the time, when there were riots in Liverpool, with black people, and if you like you could call that militancy. And Mrs Thatcher when she came to Liverpool said that it was the most frightening period of her life, she really thought that a revolution was starting when it had started in Bristol, Liverpool, Manchester and so on with black riots, and she could see it, and she thought it was the end of her days.

Sophia Hawthorne 1853

It takes a great while every day to keep so large a house as this of ours in proper order. The children dine and sup at separate hours from ours. They have their supper after our dinner; so the table has to be laid four times. Mr. Hawthorne eats a biscuit in his consulate office at noon, and I eat a morsel of bread at the children's dinner. But oh, no, dear father, we do not 'live in grand style', neither do we intend to have much company. We could not afford it; for, though so many persons at home, who might be supposed to know, account the consular income here to be so great, and the arrival of ships so abundant, they are sadly mistaken. Elizabeth wrote me last week that the number of ships that arrived from the United States to Liverpool was nearly ten thousand, from each one of which Mr. Hawthorne must receive four dollars, making at once forty thousand dollars a year. So far is this from the truth, that it is really funny and melancholy at the same time. Instead of ten thousand ships, not quite seven hundred arrive yearly from the United States here; and so, instead of the income from the vessels being forty thousand dollars, it is not quite twenty-eight hundred dollars. Most of the income comes from the invoices of the great steamers. Ten and twelve thousand dollars has been

hitherto the amount of the *whole* yearly income from whatever source, – about a quarter part of the estimate made of it. It is hoped that the business may increase; but perhaps it will be too late for us. And Mr. Hawthorne must lay aside a good part of this income, or we shall return ruined, not benefited, by this office; for he cannot write, and all that would remain for us would be the 'Wayside,' which would be a home, but not bread and butter and clothes and means of educating the children. Living is much more expensive here than at home: meat never below fourteen cents, and some kinds twenty cents; potatoes thirty cents a peck; no tea below a dollar a pound; grapes are a penny apiece, and the fruit here is not good. England cannot grow fruit, with a sun crying its eyes out every day.

Ringo Starr   2004

I told him I was stood in the John Lennon Airport. We had a bit of a laugh because it's obviously quite something to have a whole airport named after you. And I told Macca that I would settle just for having a baggage carousel named after me or something.

Lady Constance Lytton   1910

At about 3.30 a.m. or 4 o'clock, Black Maria came and we were put in. This was different from the prison vans I had hitherto seen; it was not broken up into separate cell-like compartments, but was in the form of a double omnibus, one side for men and the other for women, divided by a thin wooden partition, each side having two seats facing each other and extending the length of the carriage. There were no windows; the light filtered in only through the grated ventilators. When we got into this Black Maria there was no one but us three, but we were told to sit near the door, so Mrs. Nugent sat first, then Elsie Howey, and then myself. The jolting of the van is excessive and suggests a complete absence of springs, the noise of its passage through the streets is terrific, to the point of excluding all other sounds – a noise of thundering wheels, of jolts and jars and bumps. I have not yet made out the reason why 3.30 a.m. was selected, none was given at the time to the prisoners.

Our destination was the Bridewell Police Station, but we called on our way at the other police stations in the town, picking up whatever unfortunates they had netted during the night. We called at four different stations, if I remember right. The drive in all took about an hour, and seemed a very long one.

We had not gone far before the rumbling and jolting ceased, the door was thrown open with a sound of keys and great rattling, a shaft of light fell along the 'bus, and lit up momentarily ourselves and those who were thrown in to add to our number. These were the only moments when the occupants had a chance of seeing each other. The door then hastily closed again, darkness, jolting and noise reasserted their grim influence. Drunken voices, the smell of the gin palace, an occasional query and reply shouted through the thin wall to the men on the other side, that was all. Knee to knee, and breath to breath we sat, companions of this world of darkness, fellow-sisters of the order of the outcasts. Before we had finished, we had taken up six women in all.

John Brophy 1943

But now, standing on the top deck of the New Brighton ferry-boat, with the whole prospect of the Mersey estuary opened to his unhindered view, Charles Thorneycroft realised that his native city with its satellite towns, collectively known as Merseyside, had a life, a hard, busy, highly organised life, all its own. His first impressions could not all have been false, but here at the waterfront was an almost rhetorical contrast. Here where the ships sailed in and unloaded, loaded again and sailed out once more to all the oceans of the world, here was visible all round him a continuing magnificence. Here was no sign of lethargy or despondent regrets for the prosperities of the past. Here Liverpool was laying claim with a brawny fist its own important place in the world.

King John 1207

John, by the grace of God, King of England, Lord of Ireland, Duke of Normandy and Aquitaine, Count of Anjou, to all his faithful people who have desired to have Burgages in the township of Liverpool, greeting. Know ye that we have granted to all our faithful people who have taken Burgages in Liverpool that they may have all the liberties and free customs in the township of Liverpool which any Free Borough on the sea has in our land. And therefore we command you that securely and in our peace you come there to receive and inhabit our Burgages. And in witness hereof we transmit to you these our Letters Patent Witness Simon de Pateshill at Winchester on the twenty-eighth day of August in the ninth year of our reign.

John Wellborn Root

We sailed in a steamship called the *Mileta*, a large boat over 250 feet long and about 30 feet broad, or over twice as long and nearly as broad as Father's store was in Atlanta. You can't imagine how blue the sea nor how white and beautiful the gulls looked. After being over 15 days on the way we arrived safely in Liverpool. From the place where we anchored we could see the long line of shipping (over 7 miles in length) and the almost numberless ships that steamed or sailed through the bay. Some were being dragged through the water by curious-looking little boats called 'Tuggs'. The wharfs are built of solid granite and surrounded by tall warehouses.

As we steamed up the bay I noticed a large buoy, on the top of which was a bell, continually ringing, so as to let the sailors know where the shallow water is. The shores are lined with light-houses wherever the water is not deep enough for navigation, or wherever there are rocks on which a ship would probably be wrecked. Liverpool is a place with about 400,000 inhabitants, the streets are lined with handsome buildings and thronged with people. Cabs and drays rattle along the  street. The sun does not shine as brightly, and the climate is not as fine as that of the south, but the atmosphere is smoky and damp. Mr. Beach lives in a large house, and it is elegantly furnished. I wish very much that you, with Mother, Father, and Brother, could be here.

Quentin Hughes 1964

Quite a long time ago, when I wrote this book, I was taking an Italian professor around Liverpool. He was impressed and, after a while, he turned to me and asked, 'Do tell me, where do you get this wonderful black stone?'

Gerard Manley Hopkins 1873

At eight we sailed for Liverpool in wind and rain. I think it is the salt that makes rain at sea sting so much. There was a good-looking young man on board that got drunk and sung 'I want to go home to Mamma'. I did not look much at the sea: the crests I saw ravelled up by the wind into the air in arching whips and straps of glassy spray and higher broken into clouds of white and blown away. Under the curl shone a bright juice of beautiful green. The foam exploding and smouldering under water makes a chrysoprase green.

Derek Jewell 1963

By night they flood out into the raw mistral that rips in from Liverpool Bay; over two hundred semi-professional trios and quartets on Merseyside, trailing their electric guitars, drums, voices and amplifiers into cars and vans. From New Brighton Tower to Garston Baths the 'beat' (beat for rhythm, not beatnik) groups thump, shout, kick and tremble in pubs, clubs and church halls.

The Liverpool School of Tropical Medicine was formally opened on Saturday, 22 April 1899, by no less a person than the great Lord Lister, the inventor of antiseptic and aseptic surgery, and President of the Royal Society. He was most kind to me, and examined my specimens again with interest. Just as W. E. Henley said of him, 'His face at once benign and proud and shy' impressed me greatly – a white-haired, sweet, and patient man, not in the best of health.

From that moment a rather long correspondence began between us, in which I explained away his difficulties; and I have his letters still, with copies of mine to him kindly made for me with Sir Rickman Godlee's permission. The same evening Mr. Jones gave a banquet at the Adelphi Hotel. Many distinguished men were present – Drs. Clifford Allbutt, Church, Manson, Mott, Sir W. Broadbent, Sir R. Thorne, Sir C. Cameron, Michael Foster; and I saw for the first time Mr. Haffkine and Sir William MacGregor, Governor of Lagos – the latter left before the ceremony. Lord Lister was most kind in his references to my work.

A special ward of twelve beds had been set apart for tropical cases at the Royal Southern Hospital, and, of course, I thought that I was to be in medical charge of it. Hence when Lord Lister inspected the ward I asked the House Surgeon to give certain treatment to one of the cases. Next day I received an angry letter from one of the elder physicians of the hospital, Dr. -, for interfering with his treatment of the case. It appeared that I was not to be allowed to treat the cases because I was not an M.D.! This paralysed the teaching at the School for years, since medical men from the tropics scarcely wished to be instructed in clinical tropical medicine by people who had never been out of Britain and were nowhere known to be authorities on the subject. Verily the modern Briton believes rather in ghosts than in realities.

Illustrated London News   1847

This stupendous work has just been completed at Liverpool, for the convenience of the public; it was launched on the 31st ult., from the dock in which it was built, and then took up its station for permanent use opposite the George's Pier head. The stage was towed to her moorings by seven steamers; and on its leaving the dock works there was long and loud cheering among the workmen; and the piers were also crowded with spectators, from the Clarence to the Albert Dock.

The figure of the upper surface of the Landing Stage is very nearly that of a ship's deck, with a bow at each end. The length of the Stage is 508 feet, and its width all over 82 feet. The flooring consists of 5-inch planks, of the best pitch pine, such as is used for the same purpose in a first-rate line-of-battle ship. The planks are secured with patent compressed tree-nails, and are made perfectly tight by caulking; and, to prevent the lodgment of water, the surface is made to slope gently towards the edges. From the edge inwards, for a breadth of 16 feet, the planks are laid longitudinally, or parallel with the sides of the stage; after that, for a breadth of 18 feet, they are laid diagonally, down the centre, they again run longitudinally, and in the same order between the centre and the opposite side. Thus, much additional strength is gained, by increasing the power of resisting the shock of a vessel or other body coming in contact with the sides of the Stage.

The edges are not protected by any bulwarks or chains, as they might interfere with the passage. Massive oaken stanchions, a foot square, and secured on the inside by strong iron knees, encircle the deck, at intervals of ten feet, with low mooring-posts in the intermediate spaces, well strapped to the deck. Near each bow are four longitudinal timbers, thirty-five feet in length, to serve as mooring-bits, and bearing evidence of a capacity for sustaining the utmost strain to which the mooring-chains may be subjected.

The flooring rests upon a double tier of balks firmly strapped together, making the entire depth of the wood-work $3\frac{1}{2}$ feet. Underneath, running transversely with this substantial platform, are 39 iron pontoons, flat on the upper surface, on which the timbers rest, and cylindrical on the lower, so as to offer the smallest amount of obstruction to the flow of the tide beneath. The length of the pontoons corresponds, of course, with the breadth of the flooring; except when the latter tapers off towards the ends, they are 80 feet long, by 10 feet in width, and 6 in depth. These pontoons are connected with the wood-work by iron straps, and they can be entered by man-holes from the deck, for the purpose of being examined and repaired.

The connexion between the Landing Stage and the Pier will be by means of two iron bridges, which are now in course of construction by Mr. Cubitt, the engineer of the Stage. The length of these bridges will be 150 feet, and the width 17 feet;

one for ascending, and the other for descending.

The pontoons will always be in deep water, so that steamers will be able to come alongside in any state of the tide. The area of the deck is 4467 square yards, or nearly an acre. The tonnage, by carpenters' measurement, if 16,000 tons; upon the centre area of the deck, 40,000 persons could find standing room. There are 40,000 cubic feet of timber in the Stage. And, in the construction of the pontoons, from six to seven hundred tons of iron have been used. The draught of water is two feet ten inches, but it will be over three feet when at its proper bearings, a draught which will require a superincumbent weight of 2500 tons. The entire depth is eleven feet – namely, pontoons 6 feet, and deck 5 feet. The cost of the Stage will be upwards of £50,000, and the working of it £1500 per annum, irrespective of repairs. A lighthouse, with powerful reflectors, is erected at each end of the Stage. We have, by aid of a Liverpool paper, been thus minute in detailing the construction of this stupendous Stage, from a persuasion of the great importance of the work. Some doubt has been expressed as to the possibility of the Stage sustaining a gale of wind, and a heavy sea; others doubt the holding power of the anchors. These are matters which, however, can only be tested by time. We believe this new structure to be unmatched for its colossal proportions – and the cheapness of the work – considering its strength and magnitude.

Reverend John Johns   1847

The waves of ordinary suffering swelled at once into billows; and day after day, and week after week, they rolled and rolled upon us, with the same tumult of wild expectancy, till the heart of pity was sick, and the hand of relief was weary. Day after day, and week after week, the same crowds of applicants besieged the door of your office lobby; stairs, landing-place, and even the street outside, were thronged with eager and pallid faces, wearing every shade and variety of expression that misery can produce, or hypocrisy feign. Every tide floated in a new importation of Irish misery, and the snow was loosened from our doors by hordes of bare-footed beggars.

Linda Grant   2000

From the river the city seemed like a colossus. The sky was heavy with rain and the wind was sharp. Salt and tar were in our throats, our eyes were stinging. Seabirds were screaming in the sky and the ships' horns boomed along the estuary; behind us was the emptiness of the sea. The pilot boat went out and came back in, guiding the ships through the invisible channels in the sand and silt. Lashed to them by metal cables, the tugs hauled the leviathans into port. The city bore down on the shore, the dock brought the water into land and closed in on it four-square. Everything was immense: the warehouses, the harbour board, the shipping lines, the insurance firms, our two cathedrals, all made the skyline and beyond them our magnificent temple of Zion. The city spoke in tongues and when it didn't speak it shouted.

Henry James   1869

Liverpool Adelphi Hotel, Saturday Feb.27th
So, in fine, here I am, in the reading room of this dingy &

venerable inn, scribbling with this uncommonly bad quill pen. In health & strength I'm literally immense – c'est le mot. If you could appreciate the discomforts to wh. my tender frame has been exposed - (I mean in the way of not sleeping, you know, & cuddling about for ten days on a tossing deck with nothing worthy of the name of a seat within 3.000 miles) you would appreciate the merit of my being able to hold up my head – much more brandish my fist at this rate. The last twenty four hours have been fraught with exertion & fatigue & yet – in fact, I'm all right! As for Liverpool – que c'est bien la Vieille Angleterre. The impressions of my boyhood return from the past & swarm about my soul. On finally getting in off the ship (we'd a terribly tedious time of it) I proceeded hither in a hansom & lunched off a muffin & a cup of tea in the coffee room of this mellow & musty hotel. I don't think I ever enjoyed anything quite so much as waiting for these refreshments & gazing without at the ancient & aristocratic streets & within at the full dressed waiters. This afternoon, after a short repose, I proceeded (this is for Willy) to call on our friend Dr. Inman who lives about five minutes off, in a dim & smoky vista of a street & a house of black & corrugated brick. To my great regret he was out of town & won't be home till Monday. I don't think it worth while to wait over for him; but I'll see how I feel. If I don't wait I shall leave for London tomorrow by the ten o'clock train. – I enjoy these 1st hours of landing most deeply. The sense of change novelty antiquity & all the rest of it, lies with a most warm & comfortable weight on my soul. I'm very glad I came to England first. I foresee a rich harvest of emotions.

Carl Gustav Jung 1927

I found myself in a dirty, sooty, city. It was night, and winter, and dark, and raining. I was in Liverpool. With a number of Swiss – say, half a dozen – I walked through the dark streets. I had the feeling that there we were coming from the harbour, and that the real city was actually up above, on the cliffs. We climbed up there. It reminded me of Basel, where the market is down below and then you go up through the Totengässchen, which leads to a plateau above and so to the Petersplatz and the Peterskirche. When we reached the plateau, we found a broad square dimly illluminated by street lights, into which many streets converged. The various quarters of the city were arranged radially around the square. In the centre was a round pool, and in the middle of it a small island. While everything round about was obscured by rain, fog, smoke and dimly lit darkness, the little island blazed with sunlight. On it stood a single tree, a magnolia, in a shower of reddish blossoms. It was as though the tree stood in the sunlight and was at the same time the souce of light. My companions commented on the abominable weather, and obviously did not see the tree. They spoke of another Swiss who was living in Liverpool, and expressed surprise that they should have settled here. I was carried away by the beauty of the flowering tree and the sunlit island, and thought, 'I know very well why he has settled here.' Then I awoke.

On one detail of the dream I must add a supplementary comment: the individual quarters of the city were themselves arranged radially around a central point. This point formed a small open square illuminated by a large street lamp, and constituted a small replica of the island.

I knew that the 'other Swiss' lived in the vicinity of one of these secondary centres.

This dream represented my situation at the time. I can still see the greyish-yellow raincoats, glistening with the wetness of the rain. Everything was extremely unpleasant, black and opaque – just as I felt then. But I had had a vision of unearthly beauty, and that was why I was able to live at all. Liverpool is the 'pool of life.' The 'liver,' according to an old view, is the seat of life – which 'makes to live.'

Johann Georg Kohl   1844

I went on that same evening to Liverpool, and at ten o'clock arrived on the 'Cheshire shore,' on the south side of the Mersey, opposite to the great town itself. This 'Cheshire shore' has risen and flourished simultaneously with Liverpool, and rural houses of entertainment, and villages rich in country seats have been gradually scattered along the river side, serving to the townspeople as watering-places, and as places of residence and amusement. The town receives, likewise, a large portion of its supplies from this side of the river. The broad Mersey lies between the Liverpool people and the Cheshire shore, which for that very reason, probably, is a greater favourite with them as a place of recreation. To each little place on the opposite side of the Mersey, a steamboat plies from Liverpool as a ferry. At certain hours of the day, about twelve of these ferry steamers assemble at the same wharf to take in their several cargoes, and at a given signal they all start, scattering themselves in different directions over the Mersey, like a pack of cards over a table.

We arrived at the chief of these ferries called Birkenhead, where we and our luggage were packed with railroad speed into a steamer, and within view of the widely spreading and brightly illuminated Liverpool, we glided swiftly over the dark waters of the Mersey. Every moment the echo of the noise made by our paddles as they struck the water, announced that we were passing some stately vessel lying at anchor. These echoes increased in number as we proceeded, and traversing a forest of masts, among which lamps and lanterns were glittering like so many glow-worms in a grove, we speedily reached our landing-place, and the neighbouring hotel to which we were consigned.

Johanna Schopenhauer   1787

Liverpool is the second biggest city in England after London, although less beautiful and influential than Edinburgh. The trade and industrial activities of the city have filled its horn of plenty so that riches and luxury are to be seen everywhere you look, captivating the visitor. The rich merchants make use of their profits in a well-directed way, that is by constructing many sumptuous buildings and thus embellishing a city which wasn't that beautiful to begin with. Four new palatial 'newhouses', as the locals call them here, have just been built through subscriptions, also a nice theatre, a concert hall, a big restaurant and many charitable institutes (which is a credit to the human race); all owing their existence to the city's wealthy inhabitants. The most stunning and luxurious piece of work these efforts have achieved are the docks.

The boats lie safely in those artistic harbours, almost in the very centre of the city. Here, boats are under construction or renovated, loaded and unloaded and thieves are publicly prosecuted here. Such immense docks required scandalous manpower to achieve but are of vital importance to trade.

We didn't find the promenade which follows the shore pleasant: the turmoil, the roar of the sea, its impetuousness and its unpleasant smell, but the view of the open sea from the docks compensated for the rest. The sea embellishes the landscape, it gives an indescribable charm, even to the grey looking sands. The roar of the waves sounds like friendly voices from our motherland and we listened with melancholy.

Arthur Rubinstein   1963

I am enchanted with Liverpool and its public.

Tony Lane   1956

On my first run ashore I took the overhead railway which followed the line of the docks at a height just above the top of the massive granite dock wall. Looking down into the docks I was as amazed and delighted as every other novice to Liverpool. There were a lot of strange ships with cargoes smelling a good deal stronger than anything on my ship. Already, after only five months at sea, I reckoned that this was my world. After another eight years or so I changed my mind about seafaring – but never about Liverpool.

Stephen Leacock 1921

I pass over the details of my pleasant voyage from New York to Liverpool. During the last fifty years so many travellers have made the voyage across the Atlantic that it is now impossible to obtain any impressions from the ocean of the slightest commercial value. My readers will recall the fact that Washington Irving, as far back as a century ago, chronicled the pleasure that one felt during an Atlantic voyage in idle day dreams while lying prone upon the bowsprit and watching the dolphins leaping in the crystalline foam. Since his time so many gifted writers have attempted to do the same thing that on the large Atlantic liners the bowsprit has been removed, or at any rate a notice put up: 'Authors are requested not to lie prostrate on the bowsprit.' But even without this advantage, three or four generations of writers have chronicled with great minuteness their sensations during the transit. I need

only say that my sensations were just as good as theirs. I will content myself with chronicling the fact that during the voyage we passed two dolphins, one whale and one iceberg (none of them moving very fast at the time), and that on the fourth day out the sea was so rough that the Captain said that in forty years he had never seen such weather. One of the steerage passengers, we were told, was actually washed overboard: I think it was over board that he was washed, but it may have been on board the ship itself.

I pass over also the incidents of my landing in Liverpool, except perhaps to comment upon the extraordinary behaviour of the English customs officials. Without wishing in any way to disturb international relations, one cannot help noticing the rough and inquisitorial methods of the English customs men as compared with the gentle and affectionate ways of the American officials at New York. The two trunks that I brought with me were dragged brutally into an open shed, the strap of one of them was rudely unbuckled, while the lid of the other was actually lifted at least four inches. The trunks were then roughly scrawled with chalk, the lids slammed to, and that was all. Not one of the officials seemed to care to look at my things or to have the politeness to pretend to want to. I had arranged my dress suit and my pyjamas so as to make as effective a display as possible: a New York customs officer would have been delighted with it. Here they simply passed it over. 'Do open this trunk,' I asked one of the officials, 'and see my pyjamas.' 'I don't think it is necessary, sir,' the man answered. There was a coldness about it that cut me to the quick.

But bad as is the conduct of the English customs men, the immigration officials are even worse. I could not help being struck by the dreadful carelessness with which people are admitted into England. There are, it is true, a group of officials said to be in charge of immigration, but they know nothing of the discriminating care exercised on the other side of the Atlantic.

'Do you want to know,' I asked one of them, 'whether I am a polygamist?'

'No, sir,' he said very quietly.

'Would you like me to tell you whether I am fundamentally opposed to any and every system of government?'

The man seemed mystified. 'No, sir,' he said. 'I don't know that I would.'

'Don't you care?' I asked.

'Well, not particularly, sir,' he answered.

I was determined to arouse him from his lethargy.

'Let me tell you, then,' I said, 'that I am an anarchistic polygamist, that I am opposed to all forms of government, that I object to any kind of revealed religion, that I regard the state and property and marriage as the mere tyranny of the bourgeoisie, and that I want to see class hatred carried to the point where it forces every one into brotherly love. Now, do I get in?'

The official looked puzzled for a minute. 'You are not Irish, are you, sir?' he said.

'No.'

'Then I think you can come in all right.' he answered.

Illustrated London News 1854

This magnificent edifice (St George's Hall) will be a perennial monument of the energy and public spirit, in the nineteenth century, of the people of Liverpool; a place which, of all the cities and towns in the British Empire is surpassed only by the metropolis in magnitude, wealth and importance; and which, in the quick yet solid growth of its commercial greatness, surpasses even the metropolis itself.

John Leland 1539

Lyrpole, alias Lyverpoole, a pavid towne, hath but a chapel. Walton a iiii miles of, not far from the sea is a paroche chirch. The king hath a castelet there, and the Earl of Darbe hath a stone howse there. Irisch merchants cum much thither, as to a good haven. After that Mersey water cumming towards Runcorne in Cheshire, is Runcorne Water. At Lyrpole is smaul custome payed, that causith marchantes to resorte thither. Good marchandis at Lyrpole, and much Irish yarrn that Manchester men do buy there.

Liverpool Review 1894

Eighty thousand eyes greedily devoured every movement that took place within the vast Goodison enclosure last Saturday, when Liverpool and Everton met for the first time in the history of the clubs. Forty thousand shouting, roaring, gesticulating spectators, look you! and all League records broken, both as regards attendance and gate money! Probably there were considerably more than 40,000 present, but the financial result of £1,026 12s 10d. makes it certain that at least that number viewed the match. And anyway it was a grand sight and a great event.

****

For hours on Saturday afternoon Scotland-road was congested with vehicles of all sorts and sizes. There was an apparently endless procession of cabs and hansoms, and while the scores of trams and 'buses were literally besieged by multitudes of footballers anxious to make their way to Goodison Park. The great game had come at last, and was being duly honoured. Never before had a contest of any kind soever attracted so much attention in Liverpool as this first meeting between the rival clubs of Goodison and Anfield. The approaches to the Everton enclosure seethed with struggling humanity for hours before the event, and when at last the kick-off came, the magnificent football arena presented a spectacle imposing in the extreme. It only needed a glance at the packed masses of spectators rising tier above tier in every quarter of the enclosure to make even the hardened footballer ejaculate expressions of astonishment at the drawing powers of the great game.

Everton defeated Liverpool three goals to none. It was what 30,000 out of the 40,000 present fully expected. But probably the 30,000 did not think Liverpool would make such a gallant show against the League leaders, and Liverpool, despite their defeat, will lose no prestige by the result. On the contrary, a great many thousands of folk will be made acquainted with their abilities for the first time, and the event is more likely to bring them followers than to take followers from them. For there is no denying that they played a magnificent game. They had really quite as many chances as their opponents, and up to within the last half hour it was anybody's game. If Liverpool were a little less unscrupulous in their tactics, they would be a popular team. As it was, it did them no good whatever to injure an Evertonian to such an extent as to oblige him to leave the field, and to have at least two-thirds of the fouls which were granted during the afternoon recorded in favour of the Blues. On the whole, therefore, it is not to be denied that the best team won, that the winners played the best game, and that the win was immensely popular. Also, it was not to be denied that the losers set their opponents the toughest task they have had this season, and that altogether Everton were rather fortunate to win as easily as they did.

Edwin Lutyens   1929

I went to Liverpool and arrived just before lunch. I was shown into a large dull-gloomed room, and waited, feeling nervous and rather shy, till in came His Grace – a red biretta on his head and a voluminous sash round his ample waist....He held out a friendly hand. His pectoral Cross swung towards me, and the first words he said were 'Will you have a cocktail?'

Hugh Miller   1846

Before nightfall, after leaving Nantwich, I got on to Liverpool, and passed the night in a respectable temperance coffee-house – one of the lodging-houses of that middle grade in which, in England, the traveller is sure to meet with a great many Dissenters, and the Dissenter with a great many of his brethren; and in which both, in consequence, are apt to regard the cause of Dissent as rather stronger in the country than it actually is.

Nicholas Monsarrat 1940

Liverpool was a sailors' town, and she went out of her way to make this generously plain. From the merchant-ships lining the quays and docks, from the escorts cramming Gladstone Dock, hundreds of men poured ashore every night, intent on enjoying their short hours of liberty: they got drunk, made disturbances, thronged the streets and the public-houses, monopolized the prostitutes, seduced the young girls, and accommodated the married women – and Liverpool forgave them all, and still offered her hospitality unstintingly. It was difficult to estimate the contribution to morale which Liverpool made, during this war-time invasion; but the happy background, the sure welcome, which continued for year after year, was a memorable help to sailors, giving them something to look forward to after weeks at sea, something which could take the sting out of loneliness as well as exhaustion.

Henry Stripe

There was no railway from London to Liverpool in that day. I paid my fare as an outside passenger two days before the stage coach started, as was customary. I lent my top coat to a friend who returned it to me through Pickfords & Co, but these carriers lost it, and I had to leave without a top coat or forfeit my fare – the latter I could not afford to do.

I was at the coach in good time and choose my seat which was in the dickey with my back to the body of the vehicle, the worst position I could have taken, as you will soon see.

The coaches were large and cumbersome, carrying 6 inside and 12 outside passengers and a great weight of boxes and parcels on top, it being the only quick way of getting anything readily, such as newspapers, etc. A tarpaulin covered all the packages on the top.

We only reached Islington when it came on to snow heavily, which lasted several hours and this was succeeded by a downpour of rain which continued the greater part of the journey – the wind gradually rising until it became a furious NW gale. Between Warrington and Liverpool I fully expected the coach would be blown over, it was so top heavy. While the snow and rain continued the water accumulated in the hollows of the tarpaulin, was shot up into my neck with every lurch of the vehicle, travelled down my back and came out at the boots and I unable to prevent it, and not protected by a top coat.

I became completely numbed with the cold and had to be assisted down when the coach stopped for supper and the same next morning at breakfast. I paid for both meals but could eat nothing, but was only too glad to get near a fire to cure the numbness and to dry me. When we reached Knutsford a boy came alongside with some meat pies. I purchased one, thinking I could eat it, having eaten nothing since leaving London, but on lifting the top off I found the interior was maggoting and I threw it away. The coach was off before I could expostulate with the vendor.

The stage coach was 26 hours on the journey, which was considered remarkably quick travelling. It required at least 100 horses to bring the coach to Liverpool – there was a relay of horses about every 8 miles – the horses were much distressed by the heavy and rapid travelling. The guard's horn was blown with great gusto when approaching the places for changing – as many men being engaged in the operation as could work, to save time, for the coach had to be off without the least delay – about 2 minutes was the longest time allowed for changing.

I was thankful when the coach arrived at the Saracen's Head in Dale Street without accident for I fully expected the coach would have been blown over by the furious gale. We started from London on Friday afternoon at 1 o'clock and

 arrived in Liverpool at three o'clock on Saturday afternoon – the 17th March – St Patrick's day. Paddy in those days kept up his Saints day with great glee, by tremendous processions and drunkenness. The processions were over on my arrival, but the drinking had begun in good earnest. What with the terrific gale and the drunkenness every third person you passed being in liquor, I got perfectly disgusted with Liverpool at first sight, and greatly regretted that ever I came to it to try my fortune. I began to feel I had lost another chance of prospering, that I had done wrong in leaving London. My first thoughts were to return to the favourite great city soon as ever I had taken a survey of Liverpool. I knew I could readily obtain a situation in London – several wholesale houses occurring to my mind as – Leaf Son & Coles – Bentley Pawson & Co – and others who might be glad of my services, knowing me so well. Shakespeare's lines occurred to me 'There is a tide in the affairs of men which, taken at the flood, leads on to fortune'. I'm losing my tide by my own folly. However, the next day was the Sabbath and what a change did I see! – the wind was gone, there was a perfect calm – the sun shone brightly – the streets had cleared by the heavy rain – the shops everywhere closed – no drunkenness anywhere to be seen – but people moving briskly to their church or chapel and everything so changed for the better from the previous day that I who induced to alter my mind and be contented to remain in Liverpool where I have resided ever since.

Margaret Thatcher   1981

I'd expected tonight to talk wholly about unemployment but events in Liverpool have changed that. What happened there horrified us all. A thousand policemen embattled in one of our great cities. Two hundred injured. Riot shields and CS gas needed to defend the very men to whom we all turn for protection. Nothing can justify, nothing can excuse and no-one can condone the appalling violence we've all seen on television which some of our people have actually experienced and so many fear.

Edmund Morel   1891

After numerous failures, an introduction was obtained through an English friend in Paris, to Messrs. Elder Dempster & Co., the well-known Liverpool shipowners. Application for a clerkship resulted in the offer of a pursership on one of their steamers, trading... to the Congo. The proposal awoke sad memories and filled my Mother with dismay. She took upon herself to reply. It must have been an eloquent letter that she wrote, for it brought a second offer, this time of a position in the Company's offices at a salary of £70 a year. Acceptance promptly followed.

I entered upon my new duties at the age of eighteen – in 1891, the year of the famous secret Decree inaugurating the rubber-slave-trade on the Upper Congo. A week had barely elapsed when I was summoned to the presence of the heads of the firm to translate and explain a document in the French language. It was a *pro forma* contract drawn up by the Authorities of the Congo State in Brussels, providing for the inauguration of an occasional service of steamers between Antwerp and the Congo. From the point of view of my employers' interests and intentions the draft contained a flaw to their detriment. I pointed it out. My accuracy was challenged with a brusqueness not meant unkindly, but wounding to a high-strung and sensitive adolescence unfamiliar with Lancashire abruptness. It was resented with more vigour than discretion. For a moment it seemed as though the Congo would prove my summary undoing. But the correctness of the discovery being demonstrated, the storm blew over. The contract, amended, was signed, and I resumed my immediate duties in a department unrelated with the African Branch of the firm's activities. But this was not for long: Providence, it appeared to me, had decreed my connection with the Congo.

Frederick Law Olmsted 1850

A heavy cloud darkened the landscape, and as we emerged in a few moments from the dark tunnel, whirling out of town, big drops of rain came slanting in upon us. A lady coughed, and we closed the window. Soon the road ran through a deep cutting, with only occasionally such depressions of its green-sodded bank, that we could, through the dusty glass, get glimpses of the country. In successive gleams:

A market-garden, with rows of early cabbages, and lettuce and peas;–

Over a hedge, a nice, new stone villa, with the gardener shoving up the sashes of the conservatory, and the maids tearing clothes from the drying-lines;–

A bridge, with children shouting and waving hats:–

A field of wheat, in drills as precisely straight, and in earth as clean and finely tilled, as if it were a garden-plant;–

A bit of broad pasture, with colts and cows turning tail to the squall; long hills in the back, with some trees and a steeple rising beyond them;–

Another few minutes of green bank;–

A jerk – a stop. A gruff shout:

'BROMBRO!'

A great fuss to get the window on the other side from us open; calling the conductor; having the door unlocked;

squeezing through the ladies' knees, and dragging our packets over their laps – all borne with a composure that shows them to be used to it, and that they take it as a necessary evil of railroad traveling. The preparations for rain are just completed as we emerge upon a platform, and now – down it comes in  a torrent. We rush, with a quantity of floating muslin, white ankles, and thin shoes, under an arch. With a sharp whistle and hoarse puffing the train rumbles onward; grooms pick up the lap-dog and baskets; flaunting white skirts are moved again across the track; another rush, in which a diminutive French sun-shade is assisted by a New York umbrella to protect a new English bonnet; a graceful bow in return, with lifting eyebrows, as if in inquiry; and we are altogether crowded in the station-house.

In a few minutes they go off in carriages, and room is left us in the little waiting-room to strap on our knapsacks. The rain slackens – ceases, and we mount, by stone steps up a bank of roses and closely-shaven turf, to the top of the bridge over the cutting.

There we were right in the midst of it! The country – and such a country! – green, dripping, glistening, gorgeous! We stood dumb-stricken by its loveliness, as, from the bleak April and bare boughs we had left at home, broke upon us that English May – sunny, leafy, blooming May – in an English lane; with hedges, English hedges, hawthorn hedges, all in blossom; homely old farm-houses, quaint stables, and haystacks; the old church spire over the distant trees; the mild sun beaming through the watery atmosphere, and all so quiet–the only sounds the hum of bees, and the crisp grass-tearing of a silken-skinned, real (unimported) Hereford cow, over the hedge.

Charles Dupin   1817

Liverpool, whose commerce is much less ancient than Bristol's, stands much higher in both wealth and industry and has seized the better part of the trade of her rival. The most amazing illustration of her prosperity is that just a hundred years ago, Liverpool's trade was only one forty-second part of that of the whole country, while now it is one sixth. Liverpool has thus prospered seven times as well as the average of a country which has amazed us by the extent and rapidity of its general progress.

If we seek the causes of this unexampled growth, they may be found in her location at the seaward end of innumerable canals which pass through the most active and industrious manufacturing areas in the whole of England. So it is to Liverpool, which exports their produce, that manufacturers go to seek imported raw materials.

It was in Liverpool that the first dock in Britain was built, which enabled merchant vessels to remain afloat at all times. The docks now extend to over 200,000 square metres, about 4,000 metres lengthwise and 50 metres in breadth.

The best and most spacious docks are recently completed or still under construction. The severe commercial depression in England in 1816 has not caused work to stop. Rather has it given it a new impetus through a voluntary loan of half a million, used to employ the poor at the new docks during the winter of 1816-17.

Looking at the different docks, some older, some newer, the construction of their quays, their gates and their lift- and swing-bridges clearly shows the progress of the art of dock-building. I applied myself to working out what were the successive refinements which had been brought to these various constructions.

One realises that a great port as active as Liverpool needs large works-yards, numerous shipbuilding facilities and graving docks, workshops of every kind relating to maritime skills etc. I was an interested visitor to many of them, and I specially applied myself to recording how they differed from our own facilities of the same kind.

Mariane Della Rocca   2007

When I first arrived in Liverpool, I jumped in a cab at the airport and hurried to my halls of residence, halls I had only seen on the internet just like the city itself. I remember vividly that I was really excited in the cab, a new adventure lay before me. I had been waiting so long for an opportunity to study in England and finally I was here. All those mixed emotions of joy and a slight fear of the unknown preoccupied me so that I didn't start paying any attention to what was outside until we were getting closer to the city centre.

As I started looking through the window I saw old buildings. Not the splendid Edwardian or Victorian buildings standing proudly to remind you of a glorious past... no they were newer houses, abominations built around the 1950's-60's which thanks to time, the lack of maintenance and constant traffic had aged and decayed. I recognised it as being a symptom of all surburbs: city councils concentrate their efforts on the very centres of cities and tend to neglect the outskirts. So I kept looking out for a change in scenery.

Well, I might as well tell you straight away that I am still waiting. It never improved. Even now after a year spent in Liverpool when I think of the city I see it grey, sad, dirty and full of drunkards, especially on derby days. I have to say however that I was touched by the people who live here, the way some of them cheered me up being away from home, the easy way that you can be part of this city and its people without having to prove anything or argue your case. It is an open hearted city.

Henry Morton Stanley   1856

Was this Liverpool, this monstrous aggregation of buildings, and gloomy home of ships? Before I could answer the question satisfactorily, Liverpool was all around me: it had grown, unperceived by me, into a land covered by numberless structures of surpassing vastness and height, and spread on either side of our course. We sped along a huge sea-wall, which raised its grim front as high as a castle, and before us was a mighty river; on cither side there was an immeasurable length of shore, crowded with houses of all sorts; and when I looked astern, the two lines with their wonders of buildings ran far out towards the sea, whence we had so swiftly come.

Before my distracted mind could arrange the multitude of impressions which were thronging on me, my aunt, who had sat through all unmoved and silent, touched me on the shoulder and bade me follow her ashore. Mechanically, I obeyed, and stepped out on a floating stage which was sufficiently spacious to accommodate a whole town-full of people; and, walking over an iron bridge, we gained the top of the colossal wall, among such a number of human beings that I became speechless with fear and amazement.

Entering a carriage, we drove along past high walls that imprisoned the shipping, through an atmosphere impregnated with fumes of pitch and tar, and streets whose roar of traffic was deafening. My ears could distinguish clinks of iron, grinding roll of wheels, tramp of iron-shod hoofs, but there was a hubbub around them all which was loud and strenuous, of which I could make nothing, save that it was awful and absorbing. Fresh from the slumbering existence of a quiet country home, my nerves tingled under the influence of the ceaseless crash and clamour. The universal restlessness visible out of the carriage windows, and the medley of noises, were so overwhelming that from pure distraction and an impressive sense of littleness in the midst of such a mighty Babel, every intelligent faculty was suspended.

The tremendous power of this aggregate force so fiercely astir, made me feel so limp and helpless that again I was tempted to implore my aunt to return with me to the peace of Tremeirchion. But I refused the cowardly impulse, and, before my total collapse, the carriage stopped at an hotel. We were received by such smiling and obliging strangers that my confidence was restored. The comfort visible everywhere, and the composed demeanour of my aunt and her friends, were most soothing.

Olaf Stapledon 1913

This morning I walked through the Birkenhead docks on my way here. The men were all just going to work, hundreds of them, swarming in at the shed gates, some big and burly, some crooked and lean, some young, some old, mostly smoking little clay pipes, and clumping along in big boots like Father's over mighty cobble stones.

Nelly Weeton 1808

Being so near the shore, and just at the mouth of the river, we are much exposed to the winds, and since I came here, have experienced a great deal of rough weather. For a few days at first, the weather was so warm and mild that Mrs. H. and I frequently went and sat upon the banks for an hour or two at once, and spent most of our time out of doors. Since then, there has been one continued hurricane. Last Thursday night a storm began which continued the two following days. On Friday, several vessels were wrecked; one of them in our view. Mrs. H. and I went into a bathing machine just opposite the vessel in distress, and whilst we stood sheltered from the violence of the wind, we saw it beat against the rocks repeatedly. A croud began to collect upon the shore within a few hundred yards of the ship. A reward was offered to any six or eight who would venture out in a boat to fetch the crew –

for then the vessel lay quite down on one side, the waves dashing over the off side like drifting snow, and on the nearer side, washing over the decks and carrying away everything moveable. The men for a long time were busied in hacking at the masts, which at length fell overboard with a loud crash. A boat at length sett off, but could not reach the ship. A second time the force of the waves drove them back in spite of all their exertions. A man then boldly waded into the water till he was within hearing of the poor crew, and said something to them by means of a speaking trumpet. The boat then set off the third time, and fortunately reached the ship and took out the men, all except the mate and two black sailors, who bravely, or fool-hardily, staid in the vessel by themselves from ten in the morning than four in the afternoon. In a few minutes the crew were safely landed, and gave a shout which was heard as far as our cottage. The vessel was too high upon the rocks to sink, so that everyday since, she has been unloading, and yesterday was sold by auction on the shore for the benefit of the Insurers; and to-day two fields adjoining this house are almost covered with Irish linen, which was part of her cargo, and which they have been washing in the gutter that runs close by, to get out the salt water. She was just setting sail for the Brasils.

Reverend John Wesley 1777

Mon. 14. I preached, about noon, at Warrington; and in the evening at Liverpool, where many large ships are now laid up in the docks, which had been employed, for many years, in buying or stealing poor Africans, and selling them in America, for slaves. The men-butchers have now nothing to do at this laudable occupation: since the American war broke out, there is no demand for human cattle: so the men of Afric, as well as Europe, may enjoy their native liberty.

Paul Theroux 1982

Liverpool, it was obvious from the ferry, was full of elegant old buildings. They were heavy but graceful. The city had three cathedrals and many church spires, and just as many open spaces from the blasts of German bombs. (We live in a time of short memories. A German tourist in Liverpool told me that he found the city rather wrecked and depressing – he much preferred Scotland.) Liverpool was not pleasant – no city was – but it was not bad. It was elderly, venerable, tough, somewhat neglected, and it had a very exposed look, because it was a city on the sea, one of the few large cities in Britain that was subjected to ocean gales. That was the Liverpool look: weatherbeaten.

I had expected it to be frightening: it was known as a city of riots. But it struck me as good-humoured, and inhabited by many people as alien as I was, living more or less as they pleased in what had once been extremely fine houses: the 'Somali Social Centre' was in a cracked Georgian house. It was the most Irish city in Britain, and so the most Catholic.

The Pope had just visited and been wildly welcomed. The papal flags, yellow and white, were still fluttering from the beer signs on public houses and on streets down which the 'pope-mobile' (it was bulletproof, in spite of its silly name) had passed.

Emboldened by the apparent calm, I decided to walk from the pierhead to the black district of Toxteth, which everyone called 'Liverpool Eight'. The previous summer at about this time the district had been in flames. Most of Liverpool's 40,000 blacks lived in Liverpool Eight.

I met a lady tramp. She was more grey than white, about sixty-odd and had the self-indulgent look of the drunken duchesses who were pictured in the society pages of the *Tatler*. She wore a woolly hat. She was pulling a loaded cart and had a dog on a leash. I had never met a lady tramp with a dog. I had the impression that this was her whole household on the cart – all her clothes and furnishings. There was a stink in the cart that might have been food. Her name was Mary Wilson. She quickly pointed out that she was not the same Mary Wilson who was married to a former British prime minister.

She said she would show me the way to Toxteth if I pulled her cart for a spell. I did so and nearly wrenched my arm, the thing was so heavy. She said she had picked up some bottles. There was money in bottles if you knew where to flog them.

She took a blackened pipe from under her rags and puffed it.

'Like Harold', she said, elaborating the political connection. 'I enjoy my pipe.'

Mary's uncle and aunt had gone to the United States. They had intended to settle, but they had returned to Liverpool.

'There was a depression on at the time,' she said. 'Like this one.' She puffed her pipe. It smelled of burning rags. 'We'll never see the end of this one.'

She had the Liverpool knack of being able to speak without moving her lips.

'What do you want in Toxteth?' she asked.

'Just looking.'

'They had riots there', she said. 'They bayned the place.'

'Who did?'

'The kids!' She didn't say blacks.

Liverpool used to be peaceable, she said. It wasn't peaceable any more. It was a blewdy disgrace. It was dangerous.

But it did not look disgraceful to me. It was better than the corresponding part of New York City, near the docks in Brooklyn, although it had the same bricks, and the same pong of dirt and oil and old iron.

Mary Wilson finally shuffled away. Her little dog's claws scratched on the sidewalk like matches being struck as he trotted beside her.

Mr. Duddy, a street-sweeper I met at the corner of Windsor Street, said, 'Toxteth. Go to the cinema that's bayned to the ground, and when you coom to Princes Road tayn right.'

But I was still smiling at him.

He became shifty. 'What is it?'

As a street-sweeper, what was it like to sweep up after the riots? I asked.

'Shocking', Mr. Duddy said.

'Give me an example.'

'They baynt a car,' he said.

'A lot of property was burned, I understand.'

'They tried to bayn a skule,' he said.

'But the whole place was in flames.'

'They was poodles of petrol,' he said.

'You must have seen some amazing things.'

Mr. Duddy thought a moment, then said, 'I saw a pule of blood.'

I walked on, down Princes Road. There was shabby gentility mixed with unobtrusive ruin. There was something gothic about lovely old buildings half burned to the ground, or turned into brothels (surely door-bells labelled *Fiona* and *Janine* and *Miss Tress* meant that?) Loud music came from the open windows of the 'Nigeria Social Club' and at the 'Sierra Leone Social Club' there were fat blacks in bowler hats and shabby business suits on the steps, drinking beer out of cans. I assumed that the 'social club' was a way of evading Britain's strict drinking hours, and the names suggested not racism but rather nationalism or even tribalism – I could not imagine anyone from Upper Volta or Nigeria being welcome in the 'Ghana Social Club'.

Princes Road was a wide boulevard lined with trees. I followed it down to Granby, counting policemen – eight in a matter of minutes. They walked in pairs carrying steel-tipped canes about a yard long, the sort of weapon that usually has a poetic name, like 'wog-basher'. The policemen gave the impression of friendliness and deliberately chatted to bystanders and small children, seeming to ignore the graffiti which said PIGS OUT and *Why are coppers like bananas – cos they yellow, they bent, and they come in bunches.*

The shops on side streets had either boarded-up windows or else steel mesh grates, and the same grates sheathed the public phone-boxes. I stepped into one of these phone-boxes and called the Central Police Station and asked the information officer how many black policemen there were in Liverpool.

'Who wants to know?' he asked.

'Just a curious American,' I said.

'I should have known,' he said. 'I'll tell you something – Liverpool is nothing like America. I know about the trouble you've got over there, and compared to that this is nothing. I could give you figures -'

'For starters, how many black policemen?'

'Twelve coloured officers,' he said. And the entire force was 4600.

'*Twelve!*' I laughed and hung up.

And the 'coloured' was interesting, too. Policemen were 'coloured', convicted criminals were 'West Indian', and purse snatchers were 'nig-nogs'. But when a black runner came first in a race against foreigners he was 'English'. If he came second he was 'British'. If he lost he was 'coloured'. If he cheated he was 'West Indian'.

I kept walking. The riots had left marks on Liverpool Eight

that were visible a year later: the broken windows had not been fixed, there were signs of scorching on walls and doors, and temporary barricades had been left in place. And there were posters advertising lectures by members of the Communist Party and the Socialist Workers Party – very angry lectures, judging by the titles ('Fight Back!, 'We Demand Action!' and so forth). And yet this area was not the ruin I had expected. I had been promised a wasteland, but it was no more than fine decaying houses and rotting odours.

In a ploy to gain entrance to a house I asked a shopkeeper (Manubhai Patel, formerly of Kampala, Uganda; drygoods and sundries) if he knew of a person who might sew a button on my leather jacket. Yes, he knew a *karia* – Gujerati for black – just around the corner.

'Thanks very much,' I said.

'*Kwaheri, bwana.*'

God, I thought, that feels good. It had been years since anyone had called me *bwana*.

Mrs. Luster was from Barbados. She had lived in England since 1953, when West Indians were encouraged to leave their homes and emigrate to Britain by the Conservative government – it was thought there would be a severe labour shortage very soon. Mrs. Luster worked for about twenty years in a shirt factory, and then it closed ('all these imports from Hong King'). She was fifty-seven and been married twice; both husbands had died. Every night she said a prayer for God to send her another husband: it was no fun living alone. In her council flat, four upstairs rooms of an Edwardian terrace house (rent: nine pounds a week), she had pictures of the Queen, the Pope, Prince Andrew, the wedding of Prince Charles and Lady Diana, and Jesus Christ showing his heart in flames. Most of the pictures she had cut from magazines, but she also had postcards stuck to the wall, and five calendars, and there was so much furniture I had to walk very slowly, sliding between heavily upholstered chairs.

I asked her what she thought of Britain.

Mrs. Luster said, 'It ain't what it was.'

Not far from Mrs. Luster's house I saw three young men standing on the pavement. Their names were Pitt, Oliver and Peery. They had all been born in Liverpool and were out of work. They were all about twenty years old. When I approached them they were discussing the fortunes of a man who rejoiced in the name Funso Banjo. They claimed I knew him, but I said I had never before heard the wonderful name of Funso Banjo.

I asked them whether they thought there would be riots this year in Liverpool Eight.

Peery said, 'We already had a riot!'

'April,' Oliver said. 'Pretty big one, too.'

This was news to me. It had not been in any newspapers that I had seen.

They said that there was often trouble but that it was seldom reported by the national newspapers.

'They can't report everything,' I said. 'How big was the riot?'

They said that hundreds of people had taken part and that three cars had been burned. It had happened after the arrest of a black boy by the police – rumours had spread that the boy had been shot or beaten up by the police. The rumours were not true, but the riot had taken place just the same, and no one was sorry, because (Oliver told me) the police were always stopping black people and searching them.

I said, 'Do you think there will be more riots?'

'Depends on the police, don't it,' Pitt said.

I said, 'Then why not join the police?'

They reacted like scalded cats, and then they laughed, as if I had suggested the most improbable thing in the world.

'Just give me one reason,' I said.

'No one would talk to you,' Oliver said.

Peery said, 'You wouldn't have a friend left!'

I said that I had expected to find a devastated area, but instead this part of Liverpool seemed to me rather pleasant, with a good bus service and plenty of shops, even if they did have boarded-up windows.

Oliver said, 'It's not bad now.' And he smiled. 'But it's different when it gets dark.'

Sunset found me walking rapidly out of Liverpool Eight.

William Wordsworth 1819

You speak of this great commercial place as I should have expected. In respect to visual impression, nothing struck me so much at Liverpool as one of the streets near the river, in which is a number of lofty and large warehouses, with the processes of receiving and discharging goods.

Saranda Hajdari 2000

We are from Kosovo – we came here after two months in the camps in Macedonia. We didn't know we were coming to Liverpool until we arrived – it was a nice surprise because we knew about Liverpool Football Club. What is our favourite thing in Liverpool? Everything! Shopping, and chocolate, and bananas, fish and chips! But not sprouts – yuk. The parks are beautiful, the trees in Sefton Park – it's nice to play ball there. We have been given very nice flats to live in, very comfortable. Everyone in Liverpool has been very welcoming, kind, very friendly. They gave us so much when we arrived. We had come from a war. We had nothing – all we wanted was somewhere to sleep.

Paul McCartney 1990

It was lovely anyway, being on the banks of the Mersey, because you could see the weather coming in off the top of Wales. I'm looking across to Flint, the Dee and the Wirral and all of that. In the morning it was a bit cloudy but suddenly it was, 'It's gonna be great!' We did our sound-check and it got more and more beautiful as the sun started to go down. It's the power of the Mersey. There is a power in those rivers, the artery of life.

The life-story of our community is a long one; if it has been rightly told, it is a thrilling one too, full of strange contrasts and marvellous changes of fortune and ideas. It has not been rightly told if, at the end of it, the reader feels any disposition to glory in the colossal heaping up of wealth and the colossal increase of population. Trade may go as swiftly as it has come; the great docks may lie empty, with grass-grown wharves; the miles of cheap houses may drop to pieces in vague heaps where dockans and nettles will flourish. If that fate should come, what will be the judgement of the world upon the character and the work of the dead city? Will travellers come to Liverpool in the spirit in which we may go to Carthage, to view the inexpressive relics of a people that pursued gain with remorseless energy, and then were blotted out? Or will they come in the spirit in which we still visit Athens or Florence, to see a real city, a city whose very atmosphere enriched the lives of all its citizens, a city which, for that reason, the world can never allow itself to forget?

BIOGRAPHIES

Henry Brooks ADAMS (1838-1918) was descended from two American presidents but preferred the academic life, passing through Liverpool on an 1858 tour of Europe.

ALBERT, Prince Consort (1819-1861) sailed into the Albert Dock on 1 August 1846 on the royal yacht *Fairy*, and officially opened the dazzling new dock system.

Reverend Richard Acland ARMSTRONG (1843-1905) was a Unitarian minister who moved to Liverpool in 1885 and wrote powerfully about the poverty he witnessed.

John James AUDUBON (1785-1851) was a Haitian artist who came to Liverpool in 1826 to raise funds for his mighty book *Birds of America*, of which Liverpool Central Library has a rare copy.

Joseph BALLARD (1789-1877) was born into a Boston family who owned a livery and hack company, and sailed to Liverpool on business in 1815 through 'mountain waves.'

Lorenza Stevens BERBINEAU (d 1869) was a servant for a wealthy Boston family who sailed to Liverpool in 1851, en route to the Great Exhibition at London's Crystal Palace.

Sir John BETJEMAN (1906-1984) was Poet Laureate, and an architectural critic who championed the Georgian townscapes and civic buildings of Liverpool and Birkenhead.

Bryan BLUNDELL (1674-1756) was a master mariner best remembered for founding the Bluecoat School in 1708 which today is the oldest building in Liverpool city centre.

Henry BOOTH (1788-1869) was closely connected to the new railway all his life, working with George Stephenson on the *Rocket* and writing a history of the railway before it even opened.

John BROPHY (1899-1965) was a Liverpool-born writer who is little read nowadays but his once-popular novels include *Waterfront*, filmed in 1950 at the Liverpool docks.

William Wells BROWN (1814-1884) escaped from slavery in Ohio to become one of the first African American writers and a powerful anti-slavery speaker at home and in Europe.

The BUILDER was a British architectural journal for 'builders and constructors' which published many critiques on Liverpool buildings between 1843 and 1966.

Karel CAPEK (1890-1938) was a Czech sci-fi writer who was the first to use the word 'robot', and whose charming account of a 1924 trip to England is an understated classic.

Sir James CHADWICK (1891-1974) became physics professor at the University of Liverpool in 1935 and won the Nobel Prize for Physics the same year for his discovery of the neutron.

Dame Margaret COLE (1893-1980) spent her teenage years in Liverpool, became a pacifist during the first world war and also had a successful career as a murder mystery writer.

Captain Greenvile COLLINS (d 1694) was a naval officer who charted the seas and tides around Britain; some of his most accurate surveys were of the North West coast.

Sir Neil COSSONS (b 1939) is the chairman of English Heritage and has long championed Liverpool, since his father brought him to the city as a child to see the overhead railway.

Agnes COWPER (1874-1963) was the daughter of a Scottish sea captain who settled in Liverpool months before her birth, and sister of journalist Ernest Cowper, a *Lusitania* survivor.

Samuel Sullivan COX (1824-1889) was a widely-travelled American congressman and prolific writer who sailed to Liverpool in 1851 on the early Cunard steamship *Asia*.

Geoff DAVIES (b 1943) opened Probe Records in 1971 which became a centre for the alternative music scene in

Liverpool, running it until 1986 and also starting up record label Probe Plus.

Daniel DEFOE (1660-1731) was the writer of *Robinson Crusoe* and had such an action-packed life he could have been the original tinker, tailor, soldier, spy, and he describes several visits to the growing port of Liverpool.

Mariane DELLA ROCCA (b 1985) is from Rodez, near Toulouse, in France, and came to Liverpool in October 2005 to study English at the University of Liverpool.

Samuel DERRICK (1724-1769) was a failed actor turned writer from Dublin who ended up as master of ceremonies at Bath and Tunbridge Wells, and whose published letters include descriptions of 'Leverpoole'.

Charles DICKENS (1812-1870) was always warmly received in Liverpool, which he held 'second in his heart to London,' when he visited for his wildly popular public lecture tours.

Paul DU NOYER (b 1954) is a music journalist who has interviewed many famous pop stars but reserves his highest praise for his home town of Liverpool and its impeccable musical pedigree.

Dr William Henry DUNCAN (1805-1863) was born in Liverpool, became England's first medical officer for health in the city, and highlighted the link between poverty and disease.

Baron Charles DUPIN (1784-1873) was a French mathematician whose description of Liverpool includes a unique account of a trip on the *Etna*, the first steam ferry on the Mersey.

The EDINBURGH REVIEW was launched in 1802 and in August 1811 described the arrival of shipowner Paul Cuffee, the son of a slave, into the port of Liverpool with an all-black crew.

Celia FIENNES (1662-1741) visited Liverpool in 1698 as part of her tour through England on horseback, and memorably described the town's emergence as 'London in miniature.'

Margaret FULLER (1810-1850) was the first female journalist to work on a major newspaper, sailing to Europe for the *New York Tribune* in 1846 and stopping briefly in Liverpool.

Sir Frederick GIBBERD (1908-1984) was an architect whose best known designs are Liverpool's circular Metropolitan Cathedral of Christ the King, completed in 1967, and Harlow New Town.

Allen GINSBERG (1926-1997) was an American 'beat' poet who visited Liverpool in the summer of 1965, post-Beatles but at the height of the vibrant literary 'Liverpool Scene.'

Linda GRANT (b 1951) is a Liverpool-born journalist and

novelist whose parents were Jewish immigrants from Russia and Poland who, she says, never quite made it to America.

Robert GRAVES (1895-1985) was stationed at Litherland Army Camp during the first world war, which he survived to become one of Britain's most celebrated poets and writers.

Niall GRIFFITHS (b 1966) is a novelist who was born in Liverpool into a Welsh family, now lives in Wales and uses both places as settings in his visceral novels.

Saranda HADJARI (b 1989) came to Liverpool with her family in 1999 as a refugee from the war in Kosovo, and is now one of Britain's first UNICEF youth advisers, and studying for A Levels.

John HAMILTON (1922-2006) was the leader of Liverpool City Council during the turbulent 1980s, but it is less well known that he was a Quaker and son of a stonemason.

Edward Chambré HARDMAN (1898-1988) set up business in Liverpool as a society photographer but his best known work, *The Birth of the Ark Royal,* reflected his interests in land and townscapes.

Sophia Peabody HAWTHORNE (1809-1871) was an American illustrator and painter who lived with her husband Nathaniel (the writer and American Consul to Liverpool) in Rock Ferry on the Wirral from 1853-1857.

Gerard Manley HOPKINS (1844-1889) was a poet and Jesuit priest sent to St Francis Xavier's parish in Liverpool, where he felt miserable, 'museless' and shocked by the poverty.

Michael HOWARD (b 1941) is a politician and former leader of the Conservative Party who ran for and lost the Liverpool seat of Edge Hill twice, but has remained an ardent Liverpool FC supporter.

Quentin HUGHES (1920-2004) was an SAS commando who escaped an SS firing squad, returning to Liverpool after the war to work as a conservation architect and writer.

The ILLUSTRATED LONDON NEWS first appeared in 1842 and immediately became a hugely popular pictorial record of British social history; it also ran the first chess column.

Washington IRVING (1783-1859) was the American author of *The Legend of Sleepy Hollow*, possibly written in Liverpool where he came in 1815 to work in the family hardware firm for several years.

Henry JAMES (1843-1916) was an American writer and novelist whose fictional characters often retrace his own steps through 'the dreadful delightful impressive streets' of Liverpool.

Derek JEWELL (1927-1985) was a jazz and pop music critic for *The Sunday Times* who visited Liverpool in 1963 to write about the new musical phenomenon and later documented its demise.

King JOHN (1167-1216) is usually characterised as an inept, mean, money-grasping monarch whose treasure sank in the Wash, but he also had a hand in making a muddy pool into modern Liverpool.

Reverend John JOHNS (1801-1847) was a Unitarian minister from Devon who came to work with the poor of Liverpool in 1836, but was struck down by the 1847 cholera epidemic.

Bishop James JONES (b 1948) became Bishop of Liverpool in 1998, succeeding David Sheppard, and has supported many urban regeneration projects in the city.

Carl Gustav JUNG (1875-1961) was a Swiss psychoanalyst who famously dreamt about Liverpool and though he never actually visited, said that the dream was deeply significant.

Johann Georg KOHL (1808-1878) was a German geographer who visited Liverpool in 1844 to tour the docks and new industries, possibly to indulge in a bit of industrial espionage.

Tony LANE (b 1937) was a merchant seaman who first came to Liverpool in 1956, later 'swallowing the anchor' to become a sociology lecturer at Liverpool University.

John LELAND (c.1503-1552) was a poet and book collector who travelled the country in Tudor times for an itinerary in which Liverpool is briefly mentioned as a 'pavid town'.

Stephen LEACOCK (1869-1944) emigrated to Canada at six and had two successful careers, as a political scientist and a humourist, and wrote a comic account of his time in Liverpool in 1921.

John Winston LENNON (1940-1980) was a founder member of The Beatles whose surrealist writing was influenced by the nonsense verse of Edward Lear and imbued with a strong Liverpool lyricism.

The LIVERPOOL REVIEW of politics, society, literature and art, which ran from 1883 to 1904, reported the first football derby between Everton and Liverpool on 13 October, 1894.

The LIVERPOOL COURIER was a daily newspaper from 1808 to 1929 and described the hectic scenes at the opening of Britain's first Woolworth's store in November 1909.

Malcolm LOWRY (1909-1957) was a novelist born in New Brighton, who took to both writing and alcohol at 15, went to sea at 18, and settled in Canada though he died in Sussex.

Sir Edwin LUTYENS (1869-1844) was a British architect who was commissioned in 1929 to design the Roman

Catholic Cathedral for Liverpool, of which only the crypt was completed.

Lady Constance LYTTON (1869-1923) was a suffragette who came on a protest to Liverpool in 1910 disguised as working woman Jane Warton, was arrested and force-fed in Walton Gaol.

Sir Paul McCARTNEY (b 1942) comes from a musical Liverpool family and started writing song lyrics as a teenager before forming The Beatles with John Lennon; he retains a strong spiritual connection with his home town.

Herman MELVILLE (1819-1891) was the American author of *Moby Dick*, first sailed to Liverpool as a cabin boy in 1839, and used the experience for his earlier novel *Redburn*.

Hugh MILLER (1802-1856) was a Scottish geologist, journalist and member of the Free Church of Scotland, visiting Liverpool on an evangelical tour of England in the 1840s.

Nicholas MONSARRAT (1910-1979) was born in Rodney Street, Liverpool, moved to London with a typewriter and £40 where he slept rough and wrote the classic war novel *The Cruel Sea*.

Edmund MOREL (1873-1924) was an international campaigner who started work in Liverpool in 1891 for the Elder Dempster shipping line and was radicalised when he saw the brutality of the Belgian regime in the Congo.

Ramsay MUIR (1872-1941) was a history professor at
Liverpool University and Liberal politician who published
his *History of Liverpool* for the city's 700th anniversary year
in 1907.

Frederick Law OLMSTED (1822-1903) was an American
landscape architect who designed Central Park, among many
others, several years after seeing Birkenhead Park in 1850.

Libor PESEK (b 1933) is a Czech musician who was chief
conductor with the Royal Liverpool Philharmonic
Orchestra from 1987-1997, and who lived at the Adelphi
Hotel when in town.

John Wellborn ROOT (1850-1891) was an American sent
to Liverpool in 1864, aged 14, to escape the Civil War and
later, as an architect in Chicago, co-founded one of the
most famous practices in America – Burnham and Root.

Sir Ronald ROSS (1857-1932) was a Scottish poet and
physician who received the Nobel Prize for his work on
malaria and joined the new Liverpool School of Tropical
Medicine in 1899.

Arthur RUBINSTEIN (1887-1982) was a world-renowned
concert pianist, born in Poland, who played at Liverpool's
Philharmonic Hall in 1963 and declared himself
'enchanted'.

Johanna SCHOPENHAUER (1766-1838) was a writer born in Danzig, now Gdansk, who visited Liverpool in 1787, and was the estranged mother of philosopher Arthur Schopenhauer.

Walter Dixon SCOTT (1881-1915) was born in Kirkdale, Liverpool and was a talented writer whose life was cut short by dysentery contracted at the first world war battle of Gallipoli.

Hugh SHIMMIN (1819-1879) moved to Liverpool from the Isle of Man and became an acid-penned journalist, chronicling the social and moral ills of all classes of Liverpool society.

Sir Henry Morton STANLEY (1841-1904) left a Welsh workhouse at 15 to stay with relatives in Liverpool, sailing to America in 1858 where he immediately began reinventing himself, later famously finding Dr Livingstone.

Olaf STAPLEDON (1886-1950) was a pacifist philosopher and influential sci-fi writer born in Seacombe, Wirral, whose novels, however, languished in obscurity until the 1970s.

Ringo STARR (b 1940) was a seasoned musician in Liverpool when he joined the Beatles in 1962, though he always said that his ambition was to own a chain of hairdressers.

George STEPHENSON (1781-1848) came to Liverpool from Northumberland to work on the *Rocket* locomotive;

his letter to his son about the new railway is one of the few he ever penned.

Harriet Beecher STOWE (1811-1896) was an American abolitionist who sailed to Liverpool in 1853 for a European tour about her book *Uncle Tom's Cabin* and the evils of slavery.

Henry STRIPE (1813-1899) arrived in Liverpool in 1832 to try his luck as a 'pushing young man' and joined the metals business of shipowners John Bibby & Sons; he worked as a clerk for 46 years.

Baroness Margaret THATCHER (b 1925) is a former Conservative Prime Minister of Britain who condoned the first English use of CS gas in Liverpool during the Toxteth riots in 1981.

Paul THEROUX (b 1941) is a highly successful American travel writer and novelist but whose 1983 book about his excursions round England, where he visits Liverpool, was poorly received.

Nelly WEETON (1776-1849) was a governess born in Lancaster who lived (and died) in Liverpool and whose journals reveal a stoicism in the face of hardship and betrayal.

Reverend John WESLEY (1703-1791) was a theologian, abolitionist and leader of the Methodist movement who preached extensively around the country, making several trips to Liverpool.

William WORDSWORTH (1770-1850) is perhaps Britain's most famous poet, and spoke favourably of Liverpool although his sister Dorothy refers to an illness called 'the Liverpool complaint'.

BOOK LIST

Henry Brooks ADAMS: *The Education of Henry Adams*, Houghton Mifflin, 1919

ALBERT, Prince Consort: *The Life of His Royal Highness the Prince Consort, Vol 1*, Theodore Martin, 1875

Richard Acland ARMSTRONG: *The Deadly Shame of Liverpool, An Appeal to the Municipal Voters*, George Philip & Son, 1890

John James AUDUBON: *The 1826 Journal of John James Audubon* ed Alice Ford, University of Oklahoma Press, 1967

Joseph BALLARD: *England in 1815 as seen by a young Boston merchant; being the reflections and comments of Joseph Ballard on a trip through Great Britain in the year of Waterloo*, Houghton Mifflin, 1913

Lorenza Stevens BERBINEAU: *From Beacon Hill to Crystal Palace: The 1851 Travel Diary of a Working Class Woman*, ed Karen Kilcup, University of Iowa Press, 2002

John BETJEMAN: *Men and Buildings*, Daily Telegraph and Morning Post, 22 August 1960

Bryan BLUNDELL: *Journal of Bryan Blundell*, copy held at Merseyside Maritime Museum Archives & Library

Henry BOOTH: *An Account of the Liverpool and Manchester Railway*, 1830

John BROPHY: *City of Departures*, Collins, 1946

William Wells BROWN: *Three Years in Europe, or, Places I have seen and People I have met*, 1852

Karel CAPEK: *Letters from England*, Claridge Press, 2001

Margaret COLE: *Growing Up Into Revolution*, Longman's Green & Co, 1949

Captain Greenvile COLLINS: *Great Britain's Coasting Pilot*, 1693

Agnes COWPER: *A Backward Glance on Merseyside*, Willmer Bros, 1948

Samuel Sullivan COX: *A Buckeye Abroad; or, Wanderings in Europe, and in the Orient*, 1851

Daniel DEFOE: *A Tour through the Whole Island of Great Britain, 1724-26*, abridged and edited by Pat Rogers, Penguin, 1971

Samuel DERRICK: *Letters written from Leverpoole, Chester, Corke, the Lake of Killarney, etc*, L. Davis & C. Reymers, London, 1767

Charles DICKENS: *Letters of Charles Dickens, Vol V 1847-1849* ed Graham Storey & K.J. Fielding, Clarendon Press, 1981

Paul DU NOYER: *Liverpool Wondrous Place*, Virgin Books, 2002

Dr William Henry DUNCAN: *On the Physical Causes of the high rate of Mortality in Liverpool*, 1843

Charles DUPIN: *Memoir sur la Marine et les Fonts et Chaussées de France et d'Angleterre*, Paris, 1818, from *Foul Berths and French Spies*, Adrian Jarvis, National Museums Liverpool, 2003

EDINBURGH REVIEW: *Memoir of Paul Cuffee*, August 1811

Celia FIENNES: *The Illustrated Journeys of Celia Fiennes 1685-c1712*, ed Christopher Morris, Alan Sutton Publishing, 1982

Margaret FULLER: *At home and abroad; or, things and thoughts in America and Europe*, 1856

Frederick GIBBERD: *Metropolitan Cathedral of Christ the King, Liverpool*, Architectural Press, 1968

Allen GINSBERG: *Ginsberg, a biography,* Barry Miles, Virgin Books, 2000

Linda GRANT: *Still Here*, Little, Brown, 2002

Robert GRAVES: *Goodbye to All That*, Jonathan Cape, 1929

Niall GRIFFITHS: *Wreckage*, Jonathan Cape, 2005

Sophia HAWTHORNE: *Hawthorne and his wife, A Biography, Vol 2*, Julian Hawthorne, 1884

Saranda HAJDARI: *Liverpool: A new generation, the official guide to the city of Liverpool*, Arabella McIntyre-Brown, Liverpool City Council, 2000

Gerard Manley HOPKINS: *The Notebooks and Papers of Gerard Manley Hopkins*, Oxford University Press, 1937

Quentin HUGHES: *Seaport*, Bluecoat Press, 1964

ILLUSTRATED LONDON NEWS: *New Landing Stage, Liverpool,* 12 June 1847

ILLUSTRATED LONDON NEWS: *On the Opening of St George's Hall,* 23 September 1854

Washington IRVING: *The Voyage*, from *The Sketchbook of Geoffrey Crayon*, 1820

Henry JAMES: *The Complete Letters of Henry James Volume 1: 1855-1872*, ed Pierre A Walker and Greg W Zacharias, University of Nebraska Press, 2006

Derek JEWELL: *Beatles breaking out*, The Sunday Times, 15 September 1963

King JOHN: *Letters patent to the Steward of West Derby,* 28 August 1207, held at Central Library, Liverpool

Reverend John JOHNS: *Unitarian Mission to the Poor Annual Report*, 1847

Carl Gustav JUNG: *Memories, Dreams, Reflections*, Vintage, 1963

Johann Georg KOHL: *England and Wales, 1844*, Cass, 1968

Tony LANE: *Liverpool City of the Sea,* Liverpool University Press, 1987

Stephen LEACOCK: *My Discovery of England*, Dodd, Mead & Co, 1922

John LELAND: *John Leland's Itinerary: Travels in Tudor England, 1539-1545*

John LENNON: *In his own Write*, Simon & Schuster, 1964

LIVERPOOL REVIEW: *The Great Game, Everton versus Liverpool,* 20 October 1894

Malcolm LOWRY: *Under the Volcano*, Jonathan Cape, 1947

Edwin LUTYENS: *The Letters of Edwin Lutyens to his wife, Lady Emily*, ed Clayre Percy & Jane Ridley, Collins, 1985

Lady Constance LYTTON (writing as Jane Warton): *Prisons & Prisoners*, Heinemann, 1914

Herman MELVILLE: *Redburn, his first voyage*, 1849

Hugh MILLER: *First Impressions of England and its People*, 1847

Nicholas MONSARRAT: *The Cruel Sea*, Weidenfeld & Nicolson, 1951

Edmund MOREL: *The History of the Congo Reform Movement*, Clarendon Press, 1968

Ramsay MUIR: *A History of Liverpool*, Liverpool University Press, 1907

Frederick Law OLMSTED: *Walks and Talks of an American Farmer in England*, 1852

John Wellborn ROOT: *John Wellborn Root: A Study of His Life and Work*, Harriet Monroe, Houghton Mifflin, 1896

Ronald ROSS: *Memoirs*, John Murray, 1923

Johanna SCHOPENHAUER: *A Lady Travels, Journeys in Scotland and England,* 1803, trs Mariane Della Rocca, 2007

Walter Dixon SCOTT: *Liverpool 1907*, A & C Black, 1907

Hugh SHIMMIN: *Sunday Night on the Landing Stage* Porcupine, 15 December 1860

Sir Henry Morton STANLEY: *Autobiography*, ed Dorothy Stanley, Houghton Mifflin, 1909

Olaf STAPLEDON: *Talking Across the World - the love letters of Olaf Stapledon and Agnes Miller 1913-1919*, ed Robert Crossley, University Press of New England, 1987

George STEPHENSON: *George Stephenson: the Engineer and his Letters*, W.O. Skeat, Institution of Mechanical Engineers, 1973

Harriet Beecher STOWE: *Sunny Memories of Foreign Lands*, Sampson Low, 1854

Henry STRIPE: *Sketch of the Commercial Life of H E Stripe*, unpublished diary held at Merseyside Maritime Museum Archives & Library

Paul THEROUX: *The Kingdom by the Sea, a journey around the coast of Great Britain*, Hamish Hamilton, 1983

Nelly WEETON: *Journal of a Governess Vol 1, 1807-1811,* ed Edward Hall, Oxford University Press, 1936

Reverend John WESLEY: *The Journal of the Reverend John Wesley*, ed Nehemiah Curnock, Epworth Press, 1911-1916

William WORDSWORTH: *William Wordsworth, The Letters of William and Dorothy Wordsworth, the middle years*, Clarendon Press, 1970

ACKNOWLEDGEMENTS

We are most grateful to the following for permission to reproduce copyright work in this volume:

John James Audubon, *The 1826 Journal of John James Audubon:* reproduced by kind permission of the Estate of Alice Elizabeth Ford

Lorenza Stevens Berbineau, *From Beacon Hill to Crystal Palace*: published by the University of Iowa Press

Sir John Betjeman: © John Betjeman, reprinted by permission of The Estate of John Betjeman

Bryan Blundell, *The Journal of Bryan Blundell*: reproduced by kind permission of Brigadier Dermot Blundell. The journal is held at the Lancashire Record Office, reference DDBB 8/4

Henry Booth, *An Account of the Liverpool and Manchester Railway*: reproduced by kind permission of Frank Cass (© Charles E Lee, 1968)

John Brophy, *City of Departures:* © The Estate of John Brophy

Karel Capek, *Letters from England:* reproduced by kind permission of Continuum International Publishing Group

Margaret Cole, *Growing Up into Revolution*: Longman's Green & Co (1949)

Neil Cossons: by kind permission of Liverpool City Council

Samuel Sullivan Cox, *A Buckeye Abroad:* Rare Books and Manuscripts Library, Ohio State University

Geoff Davies, from *Liverpool: Wondrous Place:*
© Paul Du Noyer 2006. First published in UK by Virgin Books Ltd 2002

Charles Dickens, *Letters of Charles Dickens*: reprinted by kind permission of Oxford University Press

Paul Du Noyer, *Liverpool: Wondrous Place:*
copyright © Paul Du Noyer 2002, Virgin Books Ltd

Charles Dupin, *Memoir sur la Marine et les Ponts et Chaussees de France et d'Angleterre:* reprinted by kind permission of The Institution of Civil Engineers

Celia Fiennes, *The Illustrated Journeys of Celia Fiennes 1685-c.1712*: Alan Sutton Publishing, 1995

Frederick Gibberd, *Metropolitan Cathedral of Christ the King, Liverpool:* Architectural Press, London 1968

Allen Ginsberg, *Ginsberg, a biography*: copyright
© Barry Miles 2000, Virgin Books Ltd

Linda Grant, *Still Here* (2002): reproduced by kind permission of Little, Brown

Robert Graves, *Goodbye to All That: p*ublished by Jonathan Cape (1929). Reprinted by kind permission of Carcanet Press Ltd

Niall Griffiths, *Wreckage*: published by Jonathan Cape. Reprinted by permission of The Random House Group Ltd

John Lennon, *In his own Write*: by kind permission of Yoko Ono Lennon

Malcolm Lowry, *Under the Volcano*: published by Jonathan Cape. Reprinted by permission of The Random House Group Ltd

Sir Edwin Lutyens, *The Letters of Edwin Lutyens to his wife, Lady Emily:* reprinted by permission of HarperCollins Publishers Ltd © (Ed Clayre Percy & Jane Ridley) (1985)

Paul McCartney, from *Liverpool: Wondrous Place:* © Paul Du Noyer 2006. First published in UK by Virgin Books Ltd 2002

Nicholas Monsarrat, *The Cruel Sea*: published by Weidenfeld & Nicolson, a division of The Orion Publishing Group (1951)

Edmund Morel, *History of the Congo Reform Movement*: reprinted by kind permission of Oxford University Press

Ramsay Muir, *A History of Liverpool*: reprinted by kind permission of Liverpool University Press

Libor Pesek © Telegraph Newspapers, London (24 May 1997)

Arthur Rubinstein, Liverpool Philharmonic autograph book, 28 May 1963: by kind permission of the Royal Liverpool Philharmonic Archive

Olaf Stapledon, *Talking Across the World*: reproduced by kind permission of the Estate of Olaf Stapledon

George Stephenson, *The Engineer and his Letters*: reproduced by kind permission of the Council of the Institution of Mechanical Engineers

Henry Stripe, *Sketch of the Commercial Life of H E Stripe*: reproduced courtesy of National Museums Liverpool (Merseyside Maritime Museum)

Margaret Thatcher, party political broadcast 8th July 1981: © Copyright Lady Thatcher, republished with permission from www.margaretthatcher.org, the official website of the Margaret Thatcher Foundation

Paul Theroux, *The Kingdom by the Sea: a journey around the coast of Great Britain,* pp162-7 (Hamish Hamilton 1983): copyright © Paul Theroux, 1983. Reproduced by permission of Penguin Books Ltd

Nelly Weeton, *Journal of a Governess, Vol 1, 1807-11*: reprinted by kind permission of the Oxford University Press

William Wordsworth, *Letters of William & Dorothy Wordsworth, the middle years*: reprinted by kind permission of the Oxford University Press

ILLUSTRATIONS

These striking illustrations were commissioned for Mersey Minis from artist Clare Curtis, and present her unique visual response to Liverpool. Clare follows a long tradition of British printmakers with her distinctive linocuts, which are imbued with a bold, contemporary feel. Felixstowe-based Clare demonstrates her empathy with the sea with maritime patterns and motifs appearing throughout her work.

These specially commissioned icons have been chosen for their multi-layered local references.

As each volume of the Mersey Minis series is published, the growing range of limited edition prints and illustrations will be available to buy online at www.merseyminis.com.

Capstan and rope: For centuries people came to and left Liverpool by sea; these are evocative symbols of arrival and departure, also resonating with the city centre's Rope Walks district.

Trunk: Liverpool has always been a city on the move; thousands of travellers pass every month through the port, the airport and Lime Street Station, braced for a new life with their worldly possessions.

Steam train: Stephenson won the Rainhill Trials with *Rocket* in 1829, for the world's first passenger railway line (Liverpool to Manchester); classic toys Hornby Trains and Meccano, invented in Liverpool.

Cotton: Bound up with the city's fortunes – cotton picked by slaves transported by Liverpool ships, trade links with India and Egypt; even today 70% of world cotton for export is sold under Liverpool arbitration.

Music: Liverpool boasts world-class music from sea shanties to the Royal Liverpool Philharmonic; Merseybeat hit international consciousness in the 1960s, but owes its heritage to cultures from around the world.

Neptune: Roman God of the Sea, mythical feature on the city coat of arms; the planet Neptune was the final home of the highly evolved human race in local writer Olaf Stapledon's *Last and First Men*.

Oak leaves: Quintessentially English; the Allerton Oak (over 1,000 years old); timber exports from Liverpool; the district of Aigburth means 'grove of oaks'; oak timbers were used to build ships on the Mersey.

THE EDITOR

Though a land-lubber herself, Deborah Mulhearn was born in Liverpool in 1958 into a family with a typically seafaring tradition.

She left school at 16 and worked in the wardrobe department of the Liverpool Playhouse. She then went back to college, and later gained a degree in English Literature at the University of Liverpool.

After the requisite stint in London, where she worked for five years in publishing and as a journalist on the *Architects' Journal*, she returned to Liverpool in 1991 to pursue a freelance career in journalism. She writes for a wide variety of national newspapers and magazines and has contributed to several books on architecture, history and environment.

THANKS

Mersey Minis evolved from two sources: my sister Rachel Mulhearn who suggested an anthology to celebrate Liverpool's 800th birthday in 2007, and writer and editor Mary Earnshaw who thought up the 'mini' format. Two valuable starting points were *Strangers in Liverpool: Just passing through*, compiled by Adrian Jarvis, and Gladys Mary Coles' book *Both Sides of the River*.

I am extremely grateful to the following people who went out of their way to dig out books, look up dates and supply information about the writers: Karen Kilcup at the University of North Carolina; Graham Fisher and Brenda Murray from the Victorian Society Liverpool branch; Mike Doran at Liverpool Culture Company; Andy Sawyer, Special Collections and Archives, University of Liverpool Library, and other staff at the Sydney Jones Library; Andrew Brown; H Lewis Ulman at Ohio State University; Adrian Jarvis and Rachel Mulhearn at Merseyside Maritime Museum; Paul Gallagher, Museum of Liverpool Life; Roger Hull and staff at Liverpool archives and local studies, Liverpool Central Library; Thomas McConnell; Arabella McIntyre-Brown; Vincent McKernan at Liverpool Philharmonic Archives; Fiona Shaw; David and Deborah Singmaster; Beccy Turner at the Wordsworth Trust, and many more biographers, curators, librarians and archivists in and beyond Liverpool. My thanks also to Mariane Della Rocca and Adam Taylor who gave their time to work on Mersey Minis.

I am indebted to Arabella and Fiona at Capsica for seeing such potential in the idea, and to my family and friends who supported the progress of Mersey Minis through to publication.

MERSEY MINIS

LANDING is the first of five volumes in the Mersey Minis series, published throughout 2007, Liverpool's 800th anniversary year. Four volumes – LANDING, LIVING, LOVING, LEAVING – are collections of writing from the past eight centuries.

The fifth volume, LONGING, is compiled entirely of new writing from around the world, marking a beat in Liverpool's history.

To find out more about the Mersey Minis series, and the new writing competition, log on to www.merseyminis.com

CAPSICA

Capsica is an independent publishing house based in Liverpool, specialising in high quality non-fiction. If you have enjoyed LANDING, you might like to read some of these:

Liverpool: the first 1,000 years
Arabella McIntyre-Brown (Garlic Press, 2001)

Sound: the Liverpool pop quiz
Spencer Leigh (Capsica, 2004)

Heathcotes at Home
Paul Heathcote (Capsica 2005)

Have a closer look at www.loveliverpoolbooks.com